NORWICH

CITY *of*

INDUSTRIES

Nick Williams

NORWICH: CITY OF INDUSTRIES

Published by Norwich Heritage Economic and Regeneration Trust (HEART)

Norwich HEART, The Guildhall, Gaol Hill, Norwich NR2 1JS
www.heritagecity.org
© Norwich HEART 2013

Norwich HEART is a private, charitable company that strategically plans, regenerates, manages and promotes the heritage of Norwich and Norfolk, and acts as a best practice exemplar nationally and internationally for developing heritage as a vehicle for social and economic regeneration.

ISBN 978-0-9560385-5-5

Text © Nick Williams 2013
Design by Mike Jefferies Design
Project management and editing by Janet Robertson and Lindsey Roffe
Printed and bound in Great Britain by Swallowtail Print

Funded by:

CONTENTS

A B O U T   T H E   A U T H O R

Nick Williams has lived in Norwich since the age of six so considers himself very much a Norwich man. Having taken early retirement in 2007 he has taken an active interest in the history of his adopted city – working for Norwich HEART as a part-time volunteer co-ordinator. He has written the *Blue Plaques of Norwich* book and the *Norwich Trails* booklets, all published by HEART.

Prior to retirement Nick worked for Anglian Water as a technician and was also a Norwich City Councillor for some years. In 2007/08 he was elected Sheriff of Norwich – an honour he very much appreciated and enjoyed. He is married to Gill and they live at Thorpe St Andrew, along with two cats, five guinea pigs and a pond full of frogs.

N A M E S   O F   C O M P A N I E S

Throughout the book we have referred to companies using their common names, which are often in the plural, e.g. Bonds, Bullards. We have however, used the possessive 's' form where the company's brand name includes the apostrophe e.g. Colman's.

THE OTHER INDUSTRIAL REVOLUTION

Say 'Industrial Revolution' and the official, historic record defaults to Coalbrookdale and the dark, satanic mills of the North. Norwich was simply a rural market town and to suggest that it played any part in the Industrial Revolution would be as absurd as identifying it as England's second city for most of the period between the Conquest and the 1780s – which, of course, it was.

Before the Industrial Revolution, the city's provenance as an industrial centre stretched back for more than 600 years, excelling particularly in textiles – in 1714, Norwich had grown to become "the chief seat of the chief manufacture in the realm." During the 'golden age' of Norwich textile manufacture, one Worsted Damask manufacturer exported to Stockholm, Cadiz, Venice and Leipzig; Norwich goods sent to Spain were being re-exported to Central and South America, and the East India Company was taking Norwich manufactures to China.

But surely industrialisation and cheaper power sources moved the centre for textile production to the North, and Norwich lapsed into bucolic obscurity? Well, no. While the North took over Norwich's role in terms of volume, the city diversified and innovated. Specialised products, such as the Norwich Shawl, helped to maintain some textile production, whilst other industries emerged to fill the textile void. As early as 1792, James Smith produced one of the first factory-made shoes, heralding the city's largest industry and the country's largest shoe factory. In the same vein, Harmers were one of the first companies to adopt sewing machines for clothing production and produce factory-made suits.

Brewing began to move from a cottage industry to an industrial-scale process, with Norwich brewers leading the way in technical innovation and competing with, and in some cases outbrewing, London companies. This was followed closely by food processing (Colman's) and chocolate (Caleys). Engineering also emerged as an important sector with the foundation of Boulton and Paul in 1797, which would go on to innovate across a wide range of fields and eventually produce the first all-metal biplane bomber and the frame for the largest airship in the world. Other engineering companies produced a host of innovative firsts, including the first wire-netting loom in the world (Barnards), the installation of the first radar station (Mann Egerton), innovation in steam engine production (Holmes, Riches & Watts) and leading developments in electrical engineering (Lawrence, Scott & Electromotors).

On the cusp between manufacturing and the emerging service industries, the city produced the first provincial newspaper in the country and the company went on to become the largest producer of provincial newspaper titles in the UK. Jarrolds picked up the baton of printing, established here in the 1500s, and later became one of the most cutting-edge publishers in the UK. Financial services also incubated in Norwich, with the roots of the current Barclay empire and the largest life assurance provider (Aviva, formerly Norwich Union) starting here.

While most of the great industries have now disappeared, what they did endures. Norwich has always been a seedbed of innovation and it is that process of finding new ways of doing things that still continues. Whether it's the invention of the hip replacement joint or amazing strides forward in food and life sciences at the Norwich Research Park, Norwich keeps on doing different and, quite often, doing it before anyone else.

INTRODUCTION

In 1910 when social historian C. B. Hawkins published *Norwich: A Social Study* he was describing an industrial city – where the majority of the working population were employed in making goods for sale. He pointed out that Norwich had long been a centre for manufacturing – known primarily for its textile trade where 'for more than six hundred years the looms have never been idle in the city'.

A century later, Norwich has few manufacturing industries left and relies for its prosperity on the provision of education, financial services, and being a destination for shoppers from a wide area. How did Norwich become an industrial city? Geography helped – the city is linked by river to other parts of East Anglia and to the sea at Great Yarmouth; in medieval times it was at the centre of a densely populated agricultural region; it was a marketplace for agricultural and other goods, and the administrative, ecclesiastical, and social centre for Norfolk and beyond.

Within living memory, many local people were employed making boots and shoes or in the engineering and food industries. With a few notable exceptions that is no longer the case. This book focuses on the period from the early nineteenth century to the late twentieth during which the city's six major industries flourished and subsequently declined. The industries included are textiles, boot and shoe-making, brewing, food manufacturing, engineering and the Norwich drapers. The inclusion of drapers' stores may seem a bit incongruous but they were an important part of the city's commercial life, several became major department stores and could be said to have foretold the city's current role as a major shopping centre. For each major industry there is also a case study on one of its prominent firms, including several that are still in business.

For centuries the dominant industry in Norwich was weaving, producing cloth using the long staple wool from Norfolk sheep. Aided by influxes of Flemish and Dutch weavers in the fourteenth and sixteenth centuries the industry prospered and 'Norwich Stuffs' – as the cloths made were known – were sold throughout Europe. The golden age of the trade was in the late eighteenth century before its gradual decline when foreign markets were lost after 1793, and changes in fashion, plus competition from cotton cloth and cheaper Yorkshire worsteds, reduced the demand for the Norwich textiles. Parts of the industry adapted and survived – in 1901 there were as many silk weavers employed as there had been in 1839 – but largely it was new industries that came to dominate: boot and shoe-making, food processing, and iron-working and engineering. Norwich also became the regional centre for brewing.

The making of boots and shoes effectively replaced textiles as the major employer – similar dexterity was required and much of the work could be done by the worker at home. Norwich lays claim to being the birthplace of the ready-made shoe when James Smith began selling ladies shoes from his shop in the Upper Market in 1792. The industry became the city's largest employer and its factories – including one claimed to be the largest in England – dominated the city.

In the same year, food processing provided employment for around 5,000 people and was the city's second most important industry.

Over half of these were employed at the works of J. J. Colman. Attracted to Norwich by the availability of good rail links and a plentiful supply of labour, Colman's had established a large riverside factory at Carrow by the middle of the nineteenth century. They were pioneers in the production of packaged, branded, mass marketed goods such as washing blue, starch and of course, mustard.

Beer had always been brewed in Norwich, mainly for home consumption, or by victuallers for sale in their alehouses. The late eighteenth and early nineteenth centuries saw the growth of the common brewers who brewed to sell to public houses. By the end of the nineteenth century, Norwich brewers were supplying beer to public houses from Lincolnshire to Essex.

Norwich's workshops and factories contained other industries. The clothing trade was a major employer, as was transport. The Great Eastern Railway employed 900 people during the latter part of the nineteenth century, whilst engineering, printing and paper bag and box-making were significant employers. Although silk weaving dominated the surviving textile industry, Norwich firms also made cloth and brushes.

Since 1910 the engineering industry, exemplified by Boulton and Paul, and Laurence, Scott and Electromotors, has waxed and waned but Laurence Scott remains and prospers.

The city also had its homegrown financial services, although the record of the Norwich banks was a chequered one. The city was the birthplace of one of the country's largest insurance groups – started by Samuel Bignold, the Norwich Union Fire and Life Societies became a global business, now known as Aviva.

Above:
A view of
Norwich from
St Peter Mancroft
in the 1890s
showing a
profusion of
factory chimneys.

THE TEXTILE INDUSTRY

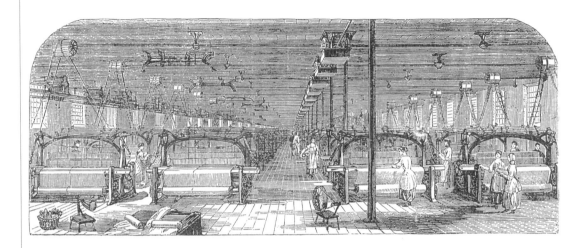

At the time of the Great Exhibition in 1851 almost a third of the Norwich workforce (male and female) was employed in the textile trade. By 1901 it was less than 7% – overwhelming evidence that (what had been) the city's pre-eminent industry for 700 years was in serious decline. Although silk-weaving continued in Norwich until the 1980s, the city's textile industry is now a distant memory.

During the fourteenth century, and probably earlier, woollen and worsted cloth was woven in rural Norfolk, with the worsted using long staple wool from local sheep. The finishing of the cloth was carried out in Norwich by the dyers, fullers and shearman. The dyers lived in the Westwick Street area, near to where dyestuffs were sold at the Maddermarket, whilst the fullers and shearmen occupied premises near Charing Cross. In 1415 the Norwich authorities enacted legislation compelling all Freemen of the city to become members of a trade association. From this date the authorities controlled the worsted industry through the various craft companies, whose wardens and other officials, elected annually, were presented to the Mayor for his approval. All woollen and worsted cloths had to be examined and, if they conformed to the association's specifications, were sealed with a token before being offered for sale. This control by the city authorities was extended in 1444 to include all worsted cloths made in the counties of Norfolk, Suffolk and Cambridgeshire.

WORSTED CLOTH

Worsted cloth production brought wealth to those engaged in its production, many of whom used it to demonstrate their piety by building and improving the city's numerous churches. Unfortunately this prosperity was interrupted early in the sixteenth century. Two devastating fires, in 1505 and 1507, destroyed several hundred houses – including those of weavers working at home. The fire compounded the effects of an economic depression which had reduced demand for Norwich cloth at home and abroad.

In 1554 and again in 1565, textile workers from the Low Countries were invited to settle in Norwich with the expectation that their technical knowledge would help revive the city's weaving industry. Known as the 'Strangers', they were Dutch and Walloons (French speaking Protestants) and included cloth merchants, dyers and wool combers, as well as weavers, with each nationality specialising in particular types of cloth. Their numbers increased quickly.

> By 1571 there were 2,850 Strangers in Norwich – men, women and children – the majority of whom were engaged in the textile trade.

By 1571 there were 2,850 Strangers in Norwich – men, women and children – the majority of whom were engaged in the textile trade. Within a decade they comprised a third of the city's population. Along with their expertise they brought their Calvinist Protestantism – many were fleeing religious persecution in the Low Countries – which was to have a significant influence on the Church in Norwich during the next century. It was not easy for them to settle and they met with some hostility – Strangers could only buy corn at the market after 1 p.m. and should they mock an officer of the Corporation they could be fined five shillings! By 1650 there were fewer than 1,500 Strangers living in Norwich – some had stayed, becoming Anglicised, but others returned to their homelands where there were once again opportunities to prosper in the textile trade.

The city authorities were determined to maintain control of the quality of the Norwich-made cloth and established search and sealing halls for those cloths made by the Strangers, in the disused church of St Mary the Less, and later in the cloisters of the former Blackfriars' church. In 1698, when the traveller and writer Celia Fiennes visited Norwich she commented 'they have beside the Town Hall a hall distinct which is the Sealeing Hall where their staple stuffs are all measured, and if they hold their breadth and lengths they are sealed, but if they are deffective there is a fined layd on the owner and a private marke on the stuff which shews its difficiency'. The sealing of cloths made in the city finished in 1710 after rioters broke open the premises and destroyed the seals and records.

THE NEW DRAPERIES

Norwich became renowned for producing light and colourful cloths using worsted spun yarn sometimes mixed with linen or silk threads. They were referred to as the New Draperies and it was these cloths, produced by the combination of the skill of the local worsted weavers and that of the Stranger weavers, which laid the foundation for the more complex cloth structures of the years to come – the 'Norwich Stuffs'. By the early eighteenth century, weaving of 'Norwich Stuffs' was concentrated in the city, with weavers working for a master-weaver. Many lived north of the river, working at their looms in upper rooms where the so-called 'weaver's windows' maximised the available light. Examples of these long windows just under the eaves can still be seen around the city.

A variety of finishing was given to cloth woven in the city. One process, extensively used and carried out in the many workshops of the hot pressers, left the cloth with a glazed surface, not only enhancing its appearance but protecting it from being soiled. The effect was achieved by first applying a dressing and then, either passing it through heated rollers, or folding it concertina fashion and placing heavy

Opposite:
Power looms
in the Willet and

Nephew factory,
possibly at
St James Mill.

heated iron plates between the folds. Great care was needed to avoid leaving scorch marks upon the cloth.

It is uncertain how much the success of the 'Norwich Stuffs' was due to the techniques brought by the Strangers but the impact of the new cloth on Norwich was immense and brought a new prosperity. Celia Fiennes commented on the quality of the Norwich crapes, calimancoes and damasks, describing them as being 'so fine and thinn and glossy' and observing that 'a man can weave 13 yards a day'. The weaving of 'stuffs' became the city's most important industry, sustaining its prosperity for over 150 years. Its success was greatly assisted by the low wages in Norwich which were about 40% less than in other textile centres. Wagonloads of 'stuffs' left Norwich almost daily to meet the demands of the London merchants who controlled overseas sales. They were widely exported to Europe and further afield. One particularly valuable market was India where the monopoly of trade was held by the British-owned East India Company.

Most weavers were reliant upon the master-weavers for their livelihoods. After serving an apprenticeship – usually of seven years – a weaver could pay a fee to obtain his Freedom and the right to trade as a weaver. The alternative was to remain a journeyman weaver working for a master. The master would provide a ready wound warp along with sufficient weft for the journeyman to weave a specific cloth on a loom at home. The loom may have been owned by the master – with the weaver paying a weekly rent. Weavers worked long hours and were reliant on the master-weaver obtaining orders from the London merchants. Lack of orders meant hardship, poverty and at times, desperation – in the 1730s at least seven weavers or apprentices hanged themselves from their looms.

THE GOLDEN AGE

The eighteenth century was the 'golden age' of the Norwich textile industry. The wealth it brought allowed some of the wealthy master-weavers to build imposing city houses such as those on Colegate owned by the Harvey and Ives families, and St Catherine's House in All Saints Green – built by dyer John Boycott as a gift to his daughter when she married John Morse. Some moved to country estates like Catton Hall – bought by Jeremiah Ives in 1788. However, this prosperity brought a new challenge – a lack of skilled weavers when they were most needed. Demand for 'stuffs' meant the most skilled weavers were much required but the casual nature of the trade meant master-weavers did not retain them when times were difficult. A few of the more far-sighted master-weavers addressed this by providing tied properties for weavers and installing looms which they had first call on.

The decline of the industry can be dated from the late eighteenth century. The wars against the French which began in 1793 were disastrous. Overseas markets were lost and could not be recovered when peace came in 1815. The loss of the Indian market in 1833 when the East India Company lost its monopoly was a further blow. The industry also faced competition from cotton cloth which was light, attractive, and easy to wash – unlike the 'Norwich Stuffs'. There was also competition from Yorkshire-made worsted which was cheaper to produce but regarded as being of poorer quality than that made in Norwich.

A consequence of decline was long periods of unemployment and hardship for the Norwich weavers and their families. The 1820s and 1830s saw weaver's wages reduced and efforts by some of the master-weavers to send work outside Norwich where it could be done more cheaply. This led to strikes such as the Camlet Weavers Strike of 1838 and attacks on individuals involved in sending work out of the city. One such case had occurred in January 1830 when John Wright, described by the local

The weaving of 'stuffs' became the city's most important industry, sustaining its prosperity for over 150 years.

press as 'one of our most considerable master-manufacturers' had vitriol thrown in his face as he arrived home one evening. Four years earlier his premises in Elm Hill had been attacked and yarn being transported to be woven outside Norwich destroyed. There were other instances of intimidation, and of work being cut from looms as the desperate weavers tried to protect their livelihoods. Some of the major master-weavers left the industry – the Gurney family investing their capital in banking, whilst the Pattesons moved into brewing.

Below: Former weaving sheds at the rear of numbers 24-28 Magdalen Street, showing 'weaver's windows' under the eaves.

In an attempt to revitalise the industry, mills were built to produce a more consistent quality of yarn by using steam power. Despite considerable investment in new mills at Lakenham, King Street and by the river at Whitefriars, it was not successful. Some of the Norwich manufacturers turned to weaving shawls. The Norwich shawl was a thing of beauty, being much acclaimed and winning prizes at international exhibitions but was time-consuming to set up, costly to weave, and subject to changes in fashion. Although Norwich shawls had a reputation for quality, other centres such as Paisley soon began printing shawls to cater for a mass market in which Norwich, with its hand-woven shawls, could not compete.

SILK AND MOURNING CRAPE

In 1856 at the behest of local master-weavers such as Henry Willet, a silk manufacturer, and John Sultzer, a cotton manufacturer in St Augustines, the Norwich Crape Company built a large factory in Botolph Street in an attempt to reinvigorate the city's weaving industry. It specialised in the production of silk mourning crape – a silk gauze which was crimped by being passed through engraved heated rollers, the degree of crimp indicating the degree of mourning being shown by the wearer. It was much in demand as bereaved family members, and their servants, were expected to wear mourning dress for a lengthy period following a death. For a time this proved profitable but changing fashions meant that by the late nineteenth century demand for silk mourning crape had declined, although the Norwich Crape factory did not close until the 1920s.

Another fabric made in Norwich was horse-hair cloth. Using hair from horses' tails imported from Russia and South America, the cloth was used to make upholstery for railway carriages, ships, furniture, and window blinds, as well as crinoline for stiffening women's skirts and bustles. There were at least five or six horse hair manufacturers, most based north of the river in or near Oak Street, including John Burrell who had premises in Gildengate and later at the Havelock steam mills off Dereham Road until the 1890s. The largest was probably Hovells in Calvert Street who were also major brush makers. At its peak, because it was woven by hand, the making of cloth provided work for weavers left unemployed by the decline in other branches of the textile trade.

Silk cloth had been made in Norwich for many years and it continued to be manufactured until the closure of the Courtaulds factory in Oak Street in April 1981. The factory was known as St Mary's Mill and had been established by Francis Hinde and Sons a century before. The company had become one of the most important silk makers in the country, but its closure effectively brought an end to 700 years of textile manufacture in Norwich.

VESTIGES

Vestiges of the city's textile industry are still visible. St James Mill at Whitefriars dominates the river, but now contains offices not power looms. Merchants' houses like Churchman House and those in Colegate are a reminder of past fortunes made from cloth, whilst the observant can glimpse 'weavers windows' on the upper floors of older buildings.

Opposite: James Churchyard, described as Norwich's oldest hand loom silk weaver when this picture was taken in 1913.

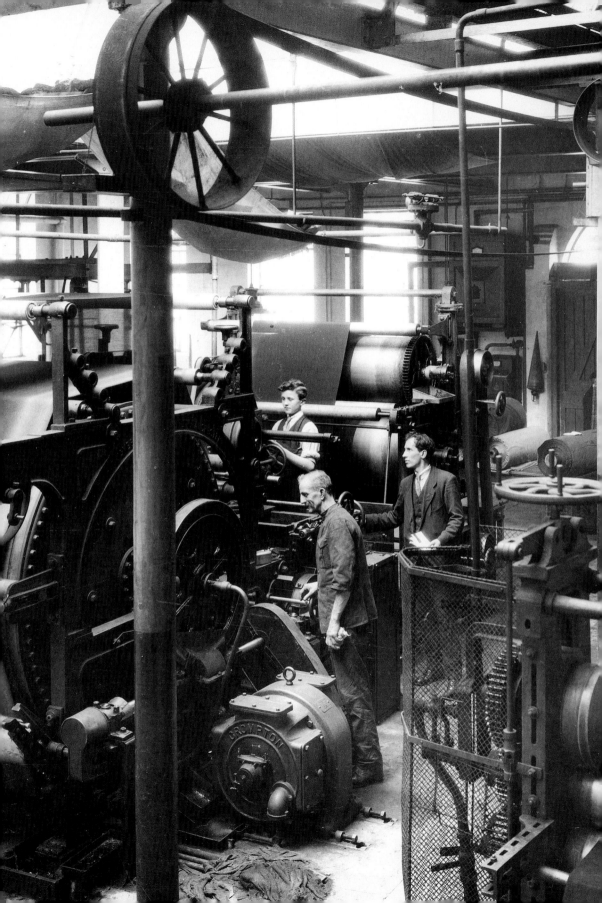

FRANCIS HINDES

The closure of St Mary's Mill on Oak Street in April 1981 brought an end to centuries of silk weaving in Norwich. Although there are references to silk vestments being used in Norwich churches during the fourteenth century there is no evidence they were woven in the city. The use of a silk warp in the weaving of bombazine is credited to the Strangers, who brought their skills to Norwich in the 1560s from the Low Countries. From then on, silk was used in a variety of Norwich-made cloth and in particular Norwich Crape – a fine silk gauze, which became widely used for women's dresses.

The name of Hinde became synonymous with silk weaving in Norwich during the nineteenth century and a visitor to their Oak Street mills around 1900 would have seen a busy, prosperous factory employing several hundred people. The raw silk was farmed from the cocoons of the larvae of the silk worm in China, Japan and India, and arrived in Norwich having been preserved in water and gum for transport. Once washed to remove the gum, and dried, it was wound by machine onto bobbins. It was then given a 'second winding' to check for flaws before being 'thrown' to insert a twist into the thread ready for weaving. The winding room was steam heated and provided with water tanks to maintain heat and humidity during the process. After weaving, the cloth was dyed, originally by hand but later by machine, to produce crape. An attempt had been made to farm silk in Norwich but the scheme, which involved the planting of several thousand mulberry bushes at Thorpe Hamlet for the silk worms to feed on, was a failure.

EPHRAIM HINDE

The founder of the business was Ephraim Hinde, born at Drayton in 1773. By 1801 he was living in the parish of St Clement in Norwich where he married Mary Norton. Within a year they had moved to Botolph Street, where he set up in business as a weaver in premises opposite St Augustine's church. When becoming a freeman in 1813 he declared he was a 'darnick weaver' by trade. Darnick or Dornix was a heavy woollen and linen cloth used for bed coverlets and carpets. He was to live in Botolph Street until his death. Two of his sons, Ephraim junior, and Francis, joined him in the business and although Ephraim junior later became a partner he preferred farming, leasing over 300 acres at Catton and living at Catton Lodge. Even prior to the death of his father, Francis was the driving force in the business, becoming a partner in 1831 – the firm then being known as E & F Hindes.

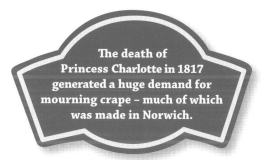

The death of Princess Charlotte in 1817 generated a huge demand for mourning crape – much of which was made in Norwich.

Opposite: Silk cloth being woven at Hinde's St Mary's Mill sometime between 1920 and 1939.

In his will Ephraim senior divided his assets between his two sons – Francis receiving houses in St Augustines Street opposite the church, whilst Ephraim junior inherited property in St Saviours, and the warehouses in St Augustines.

In the early years, yarn was passed out for weavers to weave in their homes, doing away with the need for the master-weavers, such as Ephraim Hinde, to lay out capital on building factories and employing labour directly – although he did own warehouses for the storage of raw materials and finished goods. The industry could be profitable. The death of Princess Charlotte in November 1817 generated a huge demand for mourning crape – much of which was made in Norwich – and the London merchants descended on the city, buying all available. A contemporary newspaper reported that 'during the last week all the coaches have departed heavily loaded.' Later, at a more cheerful royal occasion, Hindes made an 'opera cloak of white silk with raised velvet stripes of Humbolt-violet colour' for the future wife of the Prince of Wales, as one of the gifts from the City of Norwich at the wedding in 1863.

ST MARY'S MILL

After the death of his father in 1857, Francis brought his two sons Frank and Charles into the business, changing the firm's name to Fras.Hinde & Sons in 1878. The following year the firm moved from Botolph Street to St Mary's Mill in Oak Street (where the Silkfields Sheltered Housing scheme now stands) – a new purpose-built factory with space for all the processes necessary for weaving silk. The silk spinning and weaving process was complex, and the machinery required careful supervision – most was made on-site with maintenance carried out by mill staff. Besides crape, the firm was producing Pekin stripes, paramattas, bombazines, grenadines and other cloths.

By 1901 the firm was the most important silk manufacturer in Norwich employing several hundred people – many of them women,

employed because of their manual dexterity. The census of that year records 60 men and 643 women in Norwich who described themselves as silk weavers. C. B. Hawkins commented after visiting a silk factory (possibly Hinde's) that the women were 'a rough class of girls and women employed in throwing, on a par with confectionary workers'. That same year the business became a private limited company for what were described as family reasons – probably to minimise the financial exposure of the partners. Despite the recession following the First World War, Hindes remained a profitable business – making substantial profits even during the difficult years of 1920 and 1921. In all, it made over £210,000 in gross profits during the six years from 1918 to 1923.

Below:
Charles Hinde.
Opposite, top to
bottom: Dyeing
silk cloth;

The factory floor
at St Mary's
Mill sometime
between 1920
and 1939.

In 1924 Fras. Hinde & Sons became a public company, selling 300,000 shares at £1 each to raise money to buy out the family interest and invest in a new dye works and boiler house. By now the Hinde family had relinquished control – Frank was to die the following year aged 83 and Charles eight years later. It had assets, including freehold land, plant and stock, valued at over £180,000. It was renamed Fras. Hinde & Hardy with James Hardy, the former factory manager at St Mary's, becoming Managing Director. That same year they took over Norwich silk weavers, R L Simpson. The business expanded, building a silk weaving mill which employed 500 at Eversley Road in Mile Cross in 1928, acquiring the Oulton Silk Mills four years later, and buying James Arnold and Company, who traded as Norwich Silk Weavers Limited, in 1939. Fras. Hinde & Hardy was then one of the leading silk and rayon manufacturers in the country – producing fabric for women's dresses and lingerie.

DESTRUCTION AND REBUILDING

The outbreak of war meant that production was turned over to the needs of the armed services. Millions of yards of material were made – including silk and nylon for parachutes, fabric for barrage balloons, silks for dinghies and life-jackets, and what was intriguingly described in a post-war history of the firm as 'fabrics for secret purposes'. The war came to Hindes in April 1942 when the Oak Street works were bombed over several nights. High explosive bombs destroyed the weaving sheds and the dyeing and finishing areas. There was no loss of life but the production facilities at Oak Street were out of action for several months. The firm compensated for the loss of production by working double shifts at the Mile Cross mill.

The post-war period brought optimism about the future and a drive to support the 'Britain Can Make It' export campaign. Work began to re-build St Mary's in 1947. The new factory was to cover 48,000 square feet, be equipped with the most modern machinery, and

Below:
Demolition of
St Mary's Mill in
1983 following
its closure two
years earlier.

employ twice as many people as previously. The company was optimistic that its rayon, nylon and silk materials would be successfully exported, and developed contacts in South Africa, New Zealand, and Scandinavia. The Production Director was reported as saying 'we intend, with the aid of our employees, who really are our craftsmen, to spread our business throughout the world'. To a degree these aspirations were realised and Fras. Hinde & Hardy was a profitable business during the early 1950s when it was paying dividends to its shareholders of 12% and higher. The late 1950s saw the firm suffer substantial losses but by 1960 it was back in profit and looking to expand. In 1961 it paid out £1.2 million to acquire three smaller silk printers and the following year announced pre-tax profits of £281,000. It was the city's only remaining textile firm, employing a skilled workforce of 275 of whom 100 were men. But as the textile industry began a process of rationalisation Hindes attracted interest from larger companies.

In February 1964, an offer to buy all the shares in Hindes was made by Courtaulds Ltd who had embarked on a buying spree that was to make them one of the largest textile groups in the country. It was accepted by Hinde's chairman who controlled the majority of the shares – the takeover being completed by April 1965. A major fire in September 1979 caused serious damage to the company's Oak Street warehouse, destroying thousands of pounds worth of fabric. The following year, the factory was operating at only 30% of its capacity, leading to short-time working followed by redundancies in October 1980. In January 1981, it was announced that the factory was to close the following April with the loss of 215 jobs. Courtaulds claimed the factory was losing £1.8 million a year caused by the loss of overseas markets due to the high pound, and lack of demand for the acetate linings that had been made at Oak Street since the Courtauld's takeover. The closure effectively ended 700 years of textile manufacture in Norwich.

BOOT AND SHOE-MAKING

Since the thirteenth century, and probably well before, boots and shoes had been made in Norwich in the traditional manner. A shoe-maker would measure the customer's feet and make wooden lasts on which the shoes would be then formed. Finer shoes would be made by cordwainers – reputedly so named because they used fine leather from Cordoba in Spain. Poorer people usually made their own footwear – most wore a close fitting boot with a stocking.

Leather-working and shoe-making were governed by the craft guilds which set prices, monitored quality and controlled the number of traders. Only Freemen had the right to trade and most obtained the right by serving an apprenticeship. By the sixteenth century, boys would be apprenticed for seven years, living with their master whilst they learned the trade. They were usually paid a modest sum and in turn were expected to protect their master's interests. Apprentices were instructed in the various shoe-making processes: clicking – the cutting out of the uppers (known as clicking because of the noise made by the cutting knife as it cut the leather from a pattern); closing – the sewing together of the upper part of the shoe; sewing the sole and inner to the upper; making the heel, and finishing.

Below:
The clicking floor at Howlett and White's shoe factory in St Georges Plain in 1925.

In Norwich the apprenticeship system continued until the 1920s. It had been reinvigorated at the turn of the century in an attempt to maintain the supply of skilled workers. The boys learned pattern cutting, clicking or turnshoe making, whilst girls were trained on closing the uppers.

TURNSHOE

The more delicate shoes – such as those for women – were made by the turnshoe method. After being cut out, the leather was sewn together on a last and any surplus trimmed. It was then soaked in water and turned inside out, reformed, moulded, and allowed to dry. Shoes made in this way were flexible and fitted snugly. It also removed the need for insoles and the use of tacks. The turnshoe method required a great deal of skill and experience and used the softest, most pliable leather.

Norwich had many shoe-makers. In 1783 Chase's Norwich Directory listed 46 boot and shoe-makers in Norwich and there were no doubt many more – each serving their street or neighbourhood and working from their workshop or home. None of those listed were described as manufacturers, and almost half had premises in the market place or the streets nearby. All but one were male, the sole exception being the widow Rix in Pottergate – possibly carrying on her former husband's trade. Peck's Directory of 1802 listed 67 shoe-makers, including one boot and shoe manufacturer – Delight and Son in White Lion Street. Interestingly, three were described as ladies' shoe-makers, including James Smith. A third of the shoe-maker's premises listed were in and around the market place with a further six in the Back of the Inns. The antiquarian Blomefield records that at one time the more fashionable shoe-makers had premises on Cordwainers Row (the southern stretch of what is now Gentleman's Walk) facing the market place, catering for the wealthy and employing several staff.

Of those listed in 1783, 13 of them also appear in Peck's Directory two decades later, along with others who may well have been sons following their father's trade – an indication that bespoke shoe-making was a well-established trade that provided a good living. In 1792, James Smith opened a shop in the Upper Market selling leather and ladies' shoes. He also began selling ready-made shoes. Whilst not the first shoe-maker in England to do so, Smith is the first one known to have done so in Norwich. His modest business would become James Southall and Company, one of the city's largest shoe manufacturers, later known as Start-rite.

GARRET-MASTERS

The next 50 years saw boot and shoe-making become one of the city's most important industries. In the 1830s much of the trade was controlled by small-scale manufacturers, known as garret-masters. They would get a sample pair of shoes made up to show the wholesaler, who, if satisfied, would order more. The garret-master bought the leather, did the clicking of the uppers and the cutting out of the soles, known as bottom stuffs, and inners in their own workshops before giving out the uppers to be sewn together by the mainly female outworkers in their own homes. They would be returned to the garret-master to be passed out again to be fitted with the bottom stuffs before being finished.

At the end of the week the garret-master would be paid for the week's production by the wholesaler – allowing him to pay his outworkers and suppliers. This practice of passing out work had been inherited from the textile trade. The process was complex and time consuming – making one pair of shoes required the work of several people and much toing and froing as the materials and finished shoes were ferried from garret-master to outworker and back again. It was subject to fluctuations in demand – if the wholesaler or garret-master had no orders, the outworkers had no work, and no income, leading them to apply for poor relief.

Opposite: Interior of Howlett and White's factory in 1913 – appears to show the sewing of the uppers.

ST. MARYS
WORKS

Another hangover from the textile trade was the practice known as 'Saint Mondays,' when the Monday was treated as an extension of the weekend and little work was done.

Some of the former textile workshops were taken over for making boots and shoes such as the former Towler and Campin factory in Elm Hill which by 1883 was being used to manufacture boots. According to one historian of the city's shoe industry, by 1840 large numbers of textile workers had moved into the boot and shoe industry.

> By the late nineteenth century Norwich was a major boot and shoe-making centre.

In 1864 White's Directory commented 'During the last 15 years the manufacture of boots and shoes has become a leading branch of Norwich trade, and there are about 30 wholesale houses here employing more than 5,000 persons, chiefly in making shoes for exportation.' There was no mention of factory production as there was for other trades, but within a few years some of the 'wholesale houses' referred to, such as Willis and Williams, Tillyard and Howlett, and Haldensteins, would be making thousands of pairs of shoes a year in their factories. Many individual boot and shoe-makers remained – White listed 197 in 1864, of whom 42 were shown as wholesale manufacturers. Twenty years later there were 131 boot and shoe-makers listed. There were also 92 manufacturers, although many operated on a small scale.

Opposite: Sexton
Son & Everard's
St Mary's Works.

SHOE FACTORIES

By the late nineteenth century, Norwich was a major boot and shoe-making centre – concentrating on women's and children's shoes, although some slippers and men's boots were produced too. Shoe-making had changed from one based in small workshops and attics to an industry dominated by large city centre factories. Several of the new factory owners – such as Robert Tillyard, Henry Sexton, and later Henry Holmes, were leather merchants or curriers by trade who saw a market for their leather in making boots and shoes. Others, such as Charles Winter, were existing shoe-makers who expanded their businesses and one, David Soman, began as a cap maker.

The new factories brought mass production methods to shoe-making by utilising mechanisation. A boot riveting machine had been patented in 1810 but it would be the introduction of the sewing machine which would bring profound change to the industry in general. It was first used by Charles Winter at his St Peters Street factory in 1856. The early machines were cumbersome, requiring more than one man to operate them, but later improvements made them simpler and easier to use. The introduction of steam power, and later electricity, assisted the process of mechanisation which enabled production to be speeded up, quality to be controlled, and more shoes made. The new factories required capital, labour, and a steady supply of work to make them viable. Some of the capital came from outside the industry, such as from James Howlett, a west Norfolk farmer who invested £10,000 in the leather business owned by Robert Tillyard in Elm Hill – the forerunner of the Norvic shoe company. There was a ready supply of labour, both from the influx of people into Norwich – the city's population grew from just under 37,000 in 1801 to over 100,000 by 1901 – and from the declining textile trade. The industry began looking for new markets and by the late 1840s was exporting a large part of its output – mainly to Australia, India, Canada and South Africa. By 1913, 40% of the city's shoe production was being exported.

CHAPTER 2

Above: External
view of Howlett
and White's
factory in 1913.
Left: The former
Haldenstein and
Bally shoe factory
in Queen Street.

THE BIG FIVE

The resources required to build, operate, and improve the larger factories led to consolidation in the Norwich shoe industry, and the emergence of the five large businesses which would dominate it – James Southall and Company, Howlett and White, Haldensteins, Edwards and Holmes, and Sexton Son & Everard. Utilising the benefits of economies of scale, some took over all aspects of the manufacturing process. Haldensteins not only had several shoe factories in Norwich and elsewhere, but their engineers made the knives used for cutting the leather and their carpenters made the packing cases used for exporting their shoes. They also had a separate factory where the cardboard shoe boxes were made. The old garret-master system continued – it was useful for the factories to have additional capacity available when order books were full and there were still more than 40 garret-masters in 1910.

The big five also benefitted from a largely quiescent workforce and the low wages that were paid in Norwich. In 1906, the Norwich shoe factories were paying just under three shillings a week less in wages than the average across Britain. That year the industry employed some 3,381 workers in Norwich, of whom 1,756 were men, 462 were 'boys under 23 years of age', 850 were women and 313 were 'girls under 20'. Norwich was geographically isolated – there were no neighbouring towns competing for labour, and there was a steady supply from the surrounding area. Union organisation was weak, and some firms like Haldensteins were strongly anti-union. There was strict supervision in the work place, workers were expected to be there exactly on time – in one factory being one minute late meant the loss of 15 minutes pay, and a certain standard of appearance was expected. In the non-unionised departments wages and working conditions were poorer than those that were unionised. When work was plentiful the men would be paid at a day rate but when orders fell off it would be changed to a piece-work rate.

The National Union of Boot and Shoe Operatives had won some concessions for the Norwich employees in the 1890s but a strike called by them in February 1897 proved disastrous. Around 1,500 men went on strike for a minimum wage and stayed out for 34 weeks. In October, amidst much bitterness, the strike was called off without achieving its objective. Some 200 of the strikers were not re-employed and several of the strike-leaders were blacklisted. It would be another ten years before the Norwich shoe-workers obtained a minimum wage.

WAR PRODUCTION

In 1913 Britain was still a world power – politically powerful, and industrially successful, and the Norwich shoe industry shared in that success. Its factories employed 10,000 people and were working to capacity. Almost half the production was exported, with some factories, such as Edwards and Holmes, sending their entire output overseas. The outbreak of war in August 1914 initially made little difference. There were shortages of labour as men enlisted or were later conscripted but their places were taken by women. The factories slowly converted to war production – Howlett and White alone made almost 500,000 pairs of boots and shoes for the British Army, whilst Edwards and Holmes produced boots for the Russian Army.

There was a brief post-war boom but the 1920s and 1930s were difficult times for the industry. Export markets lost during the war were hard to regain and there was strong competition from the highly efficient American and Czech shoe industries. Nevertheless, shoe-making remained the city's dominant industry. In 1931 it was estimated to employ 17% of the city's working population, but the industry was facing severe problems. A lack of orders meant many factories were on short-time working and some were threatened with closure. Nearly 30 shoe-makers closed or were taken over, including Haldensteins, bought by Swiss shoe-maker Bally in 1933, but the major firms survived by adapting.

Sextons made American-designed shoes under licence, whilst Howlett and White concentrated its efforts on developing the Norvic brand, under which all the company's shoes would be sold. More efficient machinery was introduced and increasing numbers of women were employed.

The Second World War brought restrictions on all industries. Although initially some employees left the shoe trade to join the armed forces, by 1942 individual shoe companies were being designated as essential for the war effort. This enabled them to retain employees. Each of the Norwich shoe firms was licenced to make a certain number of pairs of shoes and allowed to employ only the staff necessary to meet the quota. To maximise the raw materials available the government ordered that half of each firms' output should be utility footwear for the general public – this was to be practical rather than stylish and made with a minimum of material. The Norwich factories, with their expertise in making women's shoes, also made footwear for the armed services – thousands of pairs for the Women's Auxiliary Air Force, the Women's Royal Naval Service, and for United States and Canadian military personnel. Air raids – which began in 1940 and continued until 1942 – badly affected production. Over 200,000 square feet of production space was destroyed and a further 116,000 partially destroyed or severely damaged. Nevertheless, the industry made the goods when needed – more than five million pairs of women's shoes, and one million pairs of children's shoes were made each year in Norwich during the war.

The immediate post-war period was a difficult one for the industry – there was a shortage of raw materials, equipment needed renewing, factories needed rebuilding, and the industry had 3,000 fewer employees than in 1939. But, within a few months of the war ending, bombed sites had been cleared and made ready for rebuilding and the industry began to recover. The use of new materials such as nylon and plastic was investigated, and new manufacturing techniques

were introduced, including the slip-lasting or 'California' process and the use of cement lasting to replace metal fasteners. Efforts were made to make the industry more attractive to potential employees. Canteens and welfare services were provided whilst improvements were made to factory conditions, including the introduction of 'Music While You Work' to combat the perception that shoe-making was a dead-end job with poor conditions and short-time working.

PROSPERITY AND EXPANSION

Shoe-making remained important to the local economy – in 1949 there were 25 companies in Norwich employing a total of 10,000 people, most of whom worked for one of the big five. After the period of post-war austerity, the late 1950s and early 1960s brought prosperity with a burgeoning young population happy to buy the women's and children's shoes made in Norwich. Production expanded to meet the need – Norvic extended their St Georges Plain complex by building the Riverside factory in 1961 and Bally moved its 750 workers from the old Haldensteins' site in Queen Street to a new purpose-built factory in Hall Road in 1969.

The Norwich shoe industry still employed 9,000 people in 1961. The city had 23 shoe factories and was confident about its future. New factories were built to meet demand – in September 1964, Meadows opened their new Fishergate works, replacing one in Peacock Street that had been demolished with the construction of the Magdalen Street flyover, and later that same month Norvic opened a new factory on Vulcan Road. On a six-acre site with room for further expansion it was part of a programme to increase Norvic production from 30,000 pairs a week to over 100,000. The city was the fourth largest shoe-making centre in the UK and was the acknowledged leader in the manufacture of ladies' fashion shoes and children's shoes.

Opposite:
Van Dal's Dibden
Road factory.

Almost all production was for the domestic market – largely to supply the shoe shop chains across the country – with only 4% exported.

DECLINE

However, this was to be the industry's swansong, as in less than a generation only Start-rite remained of the major shoe-makers and they were to cease production in the city in 2003 when their Crome Road factory closed. Norvic's collapse in 1981 symbolised the end of a once proud industry. The business had been struggling for some time and suffered a trading loss in 1980 of £1.8 million compared with a profit of £144,000 the previous year. Whilst orders for women's shoes were described as reasonably satisfactory, orders for children's shoes, which made up a large part of the company's sales, had fallen. On 1st July 1981, the company's directors announced that Norvic 'cannot now continue to trade and maintain the viability of the group in its existing form' and were calling in receivers. The receiver announced he was looking to stabilise the business but there were likely to be redundancies in Norwich where 600 were employed, and at Mansfield where Norvic employed a further 400. Within ten days, half the Norwich workforce had been made redundant and the assets – the 'Norvic' brand name, premises, plant and machinery – put up for sale. In September, the children's fitting division, the heart of the business, was bought by Ward White and moved to its Leicester headquarters. Most of the remaining workforce was made redundant and the factory on St Georges Plain sold.

Sexton Son & Everard had called in the receivers in March 1972. The company was bought by Jack Taubman who made several hundred redundancies (which were announced over the factory's public address system), closed the Beccles factory and the Fakenham finishing factory and renamed the firm Sexton Shoes. The new business employed 423 people and production was concentrated at the St Mary's factory. Sadly, the firm was to last only a further four years. In June 1976 receivers were called in.

The management commented that 'despite great efforts to sustain the company, the management sees no future… given the present difficult conditions in the British shoe industry.' Norvic offered employment to many of the 240 workers made redundant and also took over the Sexton brand but had no use for the St Mary's factory which closed on Friday 30th July that year.

Edwards and Holmes was taken over by the Florida group in 1987 and production moved to their Dibden Road factory. Bally Shoes continued until March 1997 when the Hall Road factory was taken over by a management buyout and renamed Eaton International. The company was only to last two years before calling in receivers in August 1999. Over 200 workers were made redundant and although Bally retained use of part of the Hall Road site for a time to provide accounting, customer service and repairs, shoe-making finished. At the time of writing the factory still stands – awaiting a new use.

Of the five major shoe-makers, only Start-rite was left, but in September 2003 their Crome Road factory closed and the company moved production to Portugal and India. The firm remained in Norwich having built new premises at Thorpe St Andrew to accommodate their head office, design, and administration departments. Today the only firm making shoes on any scale in the city is Van Dal whose Dibden Road factory continues a long tradition of Norwich-made women's footwear. A relative latecomer to Norwich, having its origins when Adelman Goodman bought the failing Florida shoe factory on Salhouse Road in 1936, it became know as Van Dal in 1946 and later bought the Chittock shoe factory on Dibden Road where it continues to make shoes.

Since the demise of the textile industry in the early nineteenth century, Norwich had been a shoe-making city – everybody knew someone who worked at Southalls or Norvic, and most people knew what a clicker did. The loss of such a major industry and so many jobs was a huge blow to the city's claim to be a place that made things, but was typical of the changes which were affecting manufacturing across the western world.

START-RITE

Start-rite is still based in Norwich. Its Thorpe St Andrew head office is responsible for the design of its shoes, technical development, logistics and storage, customer service, finance and management functions. Shoes designed there are manufactured in India, Indonesia, China and Portugal.

Start-rite grew, prospered, and survived because of its ability to adapt, and due to the abilities of a succession of remarkable men, related by blood or marriage, who led the company from its earliest days. Its survival also owes something to being a private, family-run business, not one driven by the short-term demands of the Stock Exchange. The firm traces its origins to 1792 when James Smith established himself in Norwich at a shop on the Upper Market. By trade a travelling leather merchant, he began making ladies' shoes, and supplying leather to the general public and to other shoe-makers. Advertising in the *Norfolk Chronicle* in 1802 he thanked his customers for their patronage, advising them that 'every effort would be made to merit their future favours.'

Norwich had many shoe-makers but Smith was unusual in that he not only made shoes to order but also held a stock of ready-made footwear. He is recognised as being the first shoe-maker in the city to do so – setting a trend that was to be copied by others and form the basis of the family business. Smith's grandson Charles Winter would go on to develop the business at a factory built on the site of his uncle's shop.

CHARLES WINTER

Upon Smith's death in 1818, his son Charles took over but died ten years later, whereupon the trustees of his estate appear to have kept the business running until Winter could assume control. Charles Winter was to play a crucial role. He was the son of William and Mary Winter, the daughter of James Smith. Described as possessing enormous energy he was credited with building up the wholesale boot and shoe business in Norwich. He developed the business massively during the 40 years he was in control – by 1851 he was employing 700 people at the factory on St Peters Street behind the Fish Market (where the City Hall now stands) – introducing machinery from the United States to speed up the process of making boots and shoes.

Right: Charles Winter.

In 1856 he brought in a sewing machine to sew the uppers, subsequently introducing machines to sew the uppers to the soles, and one to punch out the lace holes. One machine was capable of stitching soles to uppers at the rate of one pair every 60 seconds, enabling a pair of boots to be cut out, sewn and finished to a good standard within an hour. The early machines required careful tending – each having a machinist assisted by two fitters – but brought mass production methods to the industry. By the 1860s steam power was being used to drive the machinery. It would be superseded by electricity. Winter looked beyond Norfolk to sell his shoes – by 1838 he was the only Norwich manufacturer whose boots and shoes were being stocked at Marsden's Boot and Shoe Warehouse in Leeds, which advertised itself as the 'The Prime Boot and Shoe dealer in the Known World'. The firm was also exporting shoes to Canada and India.

Charles Winter was also prominent in local politics, serving as Sheriff of Norwich in 1846, Mayor in 1851, and sitting as a magistrate. He died in January 1867 at his home in Heigham Grove leaving an estate of just under £25,000. His son Charles was to die some two months later aged only 27 and control of the firm passed to James Southall.

Southall had arrived in Norwich to work for Winter around 1860, after marrying Winter's niece Marrianne Wells in London in 1857. She was a beneficiary of her uncle's will and it seems likely the money enabled Southall to purchase a share of Winter's business following his death. He managed the business for nearly 50 years until just before his own death in 1920. Initially Southall was in partnership with John Willis – the firm being known as Willis and Southall. Willis had come to Norwich from his native Gloucestershire and had at first been in business as a shoe manufacturer in Colegate in partnership with Joseph Williams. Leaving the management of the business to Southall, Willis devoted his energies to local politics – being elected to the Norwich Town Council in 1874 where he campaigned for better housing

and encouraged the council to bring the gas and water companies under municipal control. He confirmed his position in Norwich society by marrying Mary Esther Colman in 1870, the only sister of Jeremiah James Colman.

SOUTHALL

In contrast, Southall took no part in civic life but immersed himself in running the business. He expanded the St Peters Street factory into St Giles Street, and survived a potentially disastrous fire in May 1879 when machinery was destroyed and £1,000 worth of damage done. Following the death of Willis in 1888, Southall became the sole proprietor. He was instrumental in the establishment of the Norwich Shoe Manufacturers' Association, set up to deal with industrial unrest in the industry, which included demands for a minimum wage. Those demands were strongly resisted by the employers for many years. His obituary described James Southall as a man 'of considerable resource, enterprise, and untiring business application, to which circumstance is largely due the great dominance of the firm' – a fitting tribute to a man who made a major contribution to the success of the company he was involved with for over half a century.

By the end of the nineteenth century, Southalls was one of the largest Norwich shoe-makers, making ladies' shoes sold under the 'Lightfoot' and 'Fleetfoot' brands, children's boots and shoes, and light 'fancy' shoes for men. It did not make men's heavy shoes or working boots. The factory was highly mechanised with machines for almost every part of the shoe-making process. The upper machine room alone contained 20 different kinds of machines, largely operated by women and girls, where the linings were inserted. Conditions were cramped – the St Peters Street factory was spread across a number of buildings with workshops on several floors and little space for expansion.

In 1907, a new factory was built on a two-acre site at the top of Silver Road adjoining Mousehold Health. It had 25,000 square feet of production

Right: James
Southall.
Far right:
The young
Bernard Hanly.

Below: The
finishing
department at
the St Peters
Street factory.

space on a single level with adjoining warehouses and office accommodation. The following year a further two and a half acres were bought and quickly utilised to extend the factory in 1909. Some operations continued at St Peters Street until the buildings were demolished in 1936 to make way for the new City Hall.

In charge of the new factory was Bernard Hanly who had joined Southalls in 1891 as a 19-year-old. Born in Colchester, he began work in a newspaper office, then left to learn the leather trade before coming to Norwich to work at Morgan's shoe factory in the Bridewell. In 1901 he strengthened his links to the Southall family by marrying James Southall's youngest daughter Mabel, and was soon after made a member of the board of directors. By then the business had become a private limited company known as James Southall and Company.

Upon the death of James Southall in 1920, his son Frederick succeeded him as Chairman, but

retired in 1927 after what appeared to have been a series of disagreements with Hanly over the future direction of the company. Bernard Hanly was just what the business needed, being 'an energetic and strong minded leader' – essential attributes for the years ahead which would prove difficult. Active in the shoe trade's National Federation he was a strong advocate of research into new methods of shoe-making and encouraged the use of new materials. He recognised that the industry could not rest on its laurels but needed to improve its production methods and make shoes that would be attractive to consumers at home and abroad.

CHILDREN'S SHOES

It was during Bernard Hanly's reign that Southalls recognised the benefits of making shoes specifically designed for children, rather than offering what he described as 'scaled down' versions of adult shoes. To that end the company initiated an investigation into children's feet in 1928, utilising the results to design shoes that provided support and allowed sufficient space for young growing feet. The impetus for this initiative came from the retailers selling Southall shoes, who passed on the concerns of parents about the need for well-fitting shoes for their children. It was to prove the foundation of the company's long term survival. Its children's shoes became known and trusted. Recognising the benefits of a well-known brand name Southalls began selling their shoes as 'Start-rite' shoes.

The name was initially used by Bury St Edmunds' shoe shop Quant and Son on shoes made for them by Southalls. In 1921 Southalls bought the rights to the name which in time would become synonymous with the firm.

Bernard Hanly led the business through the difficult inter-war period and the early years of the Second World War. Despite the recession of the 1930s, which brought short-time working and the closure of other Norwich shoe factories, Southalls survived and by 1939 their 850-strong workforce was making 11,500 pairs a week. Although in failing health, Hanly maintained his interest in the National Federation and in the local branch of the National Institute of the Boot and Shoe Industry and, whilst not heavily involved in local politics, served as Lord Mayor of Norwich in 1940/41. He died on Saturday 13th June 1942 aged 70 – just one day after Frederick Southall, the son of his former employer.

He was succeeded as Chairman of Southalls by his eldest son James Laffan Hanly who would lead the company until his retirement 36 years later. James had joined the business in 1920 as a 20-year-old management trainee and, although he was the Chairman's son, was expected to learn the trade from the bottom up. He was dispatched to a Northampton factory to see at first hand how shoes were made and later sent out on the road to sell them. There were advantages to being the boss's son – James was sent on a world trip to investigate export opportunities and see how Southalls could increase their trade outside the UK.

Opposite: Front of Southall's factory on St Peters Street, now occupied by City Hall. Right: Bernard Hanly in his mayoral robes in 1941.

START-RITE TWINS

Taking over the company in the middle of the war was a major challenge. The company had lost much of its workforce to war service but was still expected to make its quota despite restricted supplies of leather and other materials. In 1943 James Hanly decided that the company's future lay in building upon the work done by his father by offering well-fitting children's shoes in multiple widths. Using the pre-war research, and in collaboration with schools and advice from orthopedic specialists, he initiated a nationwide survey of children's feet to establish how best to make shoes for feet that were growing rapidly. This emphasis on children's shoes was supported by a programme of training for the shop staff selling them and an advertising campaign featuring the 'Start-rite twins'. The twins became recognisable as the symbol of well-made, well-fitting shoes. Devised just after the end of the war, the twins first appeared on advertising posters on the London Underground and remained the public face of the company's promotional activities until the 1970s. They are still affectionately remembered.

The post-war period was a successful one for Southalls – confirming that the decision to focus on children's shoes had been the right one. There was huge demand and by 1949 their factories were turning out 16,000 pairs of women's and children's shoes a week. Additional production capacity was provided – Crome Road was expanded and a new factory built at King's Lynn. By 1954 the company had an annual turnover of £1 million and had phased out women's shoes to concentrate solely on making Start-rite children's shoes.

Nationally the position of the shoe industry was not so promising. Imported footwear was taking an increasing share of the home market and the number of British shoe manufacturers was declining. However, Southalls bucked this trend and continued to expand throughout the 1960s, absorbing other Norwich shoe manufacturers including Wards, Bowhill and Hubbard, and Arthur Howlett.

By 1970 Southalls was reporting record turnover, record profits, and increased exports, particularly to France. It was the largest shoe manufacturers in Norwich – employing 1,400 people who made two million pairs of shoes a year.

But it was not to last – the worldwide recession of the 1970s in the aftermath of the oil crisis brought a drop in demand for Start-rite shoes – both at home and abroad. The firm, by then known as Start-rite, having formally adopted the name in 1966, reduced output, introduced short-time working, and concentrated production at the Crome Road site – closing its other factories. Under the guidance of David White, James Hanly's nephew, who had become Chairman at his uncle's retirement in 1978 – the company returned to profitability.

James Hanly died in November 1985 and was remembered primarily for his guardianship of the family business. He had also been a director of Norwich City Football Club for many years. At his death Start-rite was still a major shoe-maker – employing 700 people who made 1.5 million pairs of shoes each year at the Norwich factory.

Start-rite no longer makes shoes in Norwich. In July 2003, having been forced to shed hundreds of jobs in the previous few years, the company announced that production would be moved abroad and the Crome Road factory would close. The previous 20 years had been a difficult time for British shoe manufacturers. Imports had continued to take more of the British market, whilst a strong pound made exports expensive. Despite these difficulties Start-rite had weathered the storm but the time came when it was no longer viable to continue making shoes in Norwich. The Chairman Peter Lamble – great nephew of James Hanly – spelt out the reasons: 'the price of making shoes is higher than elsewhere and we need to remain competitive'. He also highlighted another contributory factor – the collapse of the infrastructure necessary to sustain shoe-making – 'we can't buy soles to stick on the shoes, lasts to shape the shoes and buckles to put on the bars... We make a lot of shoes for the export market, and we find ourselves importing 100% of the components, processing them here and exporting them elsewhere'. At the time of the announcement there were only 28 people working in the 28,000 square foot Crome Road factory.

The Crome Road factory was later demolished and replaced by housing – leaving only the factory frontage as a reminder of almost a century of shoe-making on the site.

Left: Shoes racked and ready to go at the Southall factory in 1920.

BREWING

Beer has been brewed for thousands of years – the techniques involved were known to the early civilisations of Mesopotamia and Egypt, the Celts and Saxons in Britain, and by the early inhabitants of Norwich.

In the medieval period, ale – known as small beer and made without hops – was drunk in great quantities by all. As its names implies it was very low in alcoholic content – about 2% – so could be drunk without everybody being permanently intoxicated. Stronger ales were brewed for special occasions such as festivals.

The ale was brewed to be consumed within a short time as it did not keep well. Large households made it for their own use, victuallers (innkeepers who brewed on their own premises) brewed for sale to their customers, and large institutions, such as priories, monasteries and private estates would have brew houses to provide beer for residents and visitors. Norwich Cathedral had a brew house in The Close where numbers 31 to 34 now stand. Many victuallers often had a second occupation, leaving the brewing to their wives.

HOPS

The use of hops enabled beer to be brewed. The addition of hops not only gave it a distinctive flavour but acted as a preservative – enabling it to be stored and transported. By the sixteenth century hops was widely used but may have been in use in Norwich much earlier, as hop seeds were discovered during an archaeological excavation of a twelfth-century riverside site at Whitefriars, where trading ships would have unloaded their goods. However, hops proved difficult to grow successfully in Norfolk.

Above: Steward and Patteson's Pockthorpe brewery, photographed in 1974.

The basic process of brewing has remained the same for hundreds of years. The barley is malted by being soaked in water to convert the starch into sugar, then dried. Next it is crushed and mixed with hot water to produce the wort which is then boiled and the hops added. When the wort has been cooled yeast is added to begin the process of fermentation – this converts the glucose in the wort to ethyl alcohol and carbon dioxide. When the process of fermentation is complete the beer is made.

Up to and after the Middle Ages, brewing was a small-scale domestic industry where the majority of brewers were women known as alewives – in one area of England it was estimated that over 90% of the brewers were women. Many were the wives of craftsmen – brewing for their own household and selling any surplus. It was a major task – it has been estimated that a medium-sized household in the sixteenth century would use about 200 gallons of ale a month and a domestic brew would take around 15 hours to complete. Women brewers came from across the social spectrum. In thirteenth-century Norwich it included the wife of one of the city's bailiffs, and Katherine Hill – a single woman who was fined repeatedly for breaches of the regulations governing the brewing of ale.

LICENSING

In 1552 common alehouses and 'tippling houses' were required to be licenced by the local Justices of the Peace. This was the beginning of a licensing system that continues to this day. The distinction between alehouses and tippling houses is not completely clear but it seems likely that tippling houses may have sold beer but not brewed it, whereas alehouses did both.

Beer and ale were widely drunk – both at home and in inns, taverns and alehouses – the three types of drinking establishments in the medieval period. The inn had traditionally developed to serve the traveller, largely replacing the hospitality provided by the large religious houses and the homes of the nobility.

In 1577 a survey recorded more than 3,500 inns across England. Taverns were fewer in number and tended to be places where food and wine were served. Alehouses existed in profusion and were drinking places for the so-called lower orders – the same survey recorded over 20,000. Within a little over a hundred years this figure had more than doubled to about 58,000 – estimated to be one for every 90 of the country's inhabitants. The term public house came into use by the late seventeenth century, to describe inns and the larger alehouses and subsequently was used to describe most licenced drinking places.

Regulations had been introduced in the thirteenth century by the Assize of Bread and Ale to control the price and quality of ale. It was later priced according to its strength. It seems likely that such regulations were also intended to combat the social ills associated with alcohol, such as drunkenness and brothel keeping. There were further attempts at controlling the trade. In Norwich during the seventeenth century an Alderman had to approve applications for any tavern licences in his ward in advance of them being granted, whilst the constables were responsible for identifying unlicenced premises selling beer. Anybody found keeping unlicenced premises could be fined or whipped; a repeat offence could see them confined in the Bridewell.

COMMERCIAL BREWERS

The sixteenth century saw the emergence of commercial or 'common brewers' who brewed on a larger scale than before and to sell rather than for their own consumption. Brewing now became a male-dominated trade and those involved sort to protect their investment by lobbying government to restrict brewing to a favoured few. There were proclamations forbidding victuallers selling beer other than that bought from a licenced brewer but it seems likely that the regulations were widely flouted.

The common brewers would eventually come to dominate the trade and many became wealthy and influential. One of the earliest was Thomas Codde, who in 1549 became the first brewer to be elected Mayor of Norwich. The city's taxation records show that brewers were a force within Norwich – when taxation was raised in 1645 to support the Parliamentary army, and again in 1665 to repair the city walls, many of those taxed were brewers – nine in 1645 and 13 in 1665. During the period from 1620 to 1690, 14 of those selected as magistrates were brewers, only grocers and merchants provided more.

The number of common brewers in England increased substantially during the eighteenth century from 746 in 1700 to 1,382 by 1799; a Norwich trade directory for 1783 listed nine breweries in the city alone. The same period saw a reduction in the number of victuallers from just over 39,000 in 1700 to 23,000 a hundred years later. The success and increasing wealth of the common brewers attracted the interest of government and by the early eighteenth century the duty on ale and beer comprised a quarter of all public revenues.

Wealthy Norwich merchants began taking an interest in brewing. Some – such as John Patteson – moved from the declining textile industry. In 1793 he bought Greeve's Pockthorpe brewery, reportedly to provide a business for his oldest son. As Steward & Patteson, the firm would become Norwich's largest brewers. Patteson swiftly expanded the business, buying Beevor's brewery and malthouses in 1794, and Postle's brewery the year after, whilst also acquiring a number of public houses. Other prominent Norwich brewers at that time included Stackhouse Tompson and Company in King Street, and Charles Weston of St Georges Bridge Street. Weston is also credited with being the city's first banker.

BETTER BEER

Technical developments during the late eighteenth century gave brewers greater control of the brewing process, enabling beer of a more consistent quality to be produced. The two most important were the development of the thermometer which enabled the temperature to be monitored during fermentation, and the hydrometer which allowed the specific gravity of beer to be determined and thus controlled. The introduction of steam power to drive pumps and grist mills for grinding malt made brewing possible on a larger scale than before. Brewing was not without its hazards, as demonstrated in May 1845 when Walter Morgan was found drowned in a fermentation tun at the King Street brewery recently taken over by his family. Walter was learning the trade and had been asked to take samples from the tun. It appears he was overcome by the 'carbonic gas' given off, overbalanced and fell into the tun.

By the end of the eighteenth century there were at least nine major Norwich brewers. They produced mainly light beer, porter – a heavier longer-lasting beer – and 'Norwich Nog', and sold bottled and cask beer brewed elsewhere. Nog was unique to Norwich – it was a strong brown beer which was stored in vats for a period before sale. It was claimed that it was so strong that 'only the most hardened drinker could walk through a doorway without touching the door posts' after drinking a quart. Weston's in particular was renowned for their Norwich Nog. Within 40 years the number of brewers had more than doubled. Pigot's Directory of 1839 lists 19 – including some who were to later dominate the industry such as Bullards, Youngs, Crawshays, and Steward & Patteson; an indication that there was money to be made from brewing beer in a city with a growing population. There was good reason for their optimism as brewing was probably the most stable and lucrative trade in Norwich during the nineteenth century.

Increasingly, the brewers were now part of the city's ruling elite, providing Sheriffs and Mayors on a frequent basis. Nockold Tompson, who owned breweries in Orford Place and King Street, was Mayor in 1759. Several of the Patteson family held civic office during the nineteenth century, whilst Harry Bullard, described as 'probably the best known of all Norwich citizens of his time', was Mayor three times. The last brewer to hold the mayoralty was Walter Riley, Lord Mayor in 1935, the head brewer at Morgan's King Street brewery.

THE BEER ACT

The dominance of the common brewers did not go unchallenged. The Beer Act of 1830 removed the duty on beer and permitted any person to sell it providing they obtained an Excise licence costing two guineas. The power to issue and revoke licences was also taken away from the local Justices of the Peace. The only restrictions on the new beer houses were that they could not open before 4 a.m., had to close by 10 p.m., had to remain closed during certain church services, and were not permitted to sell wines and spirits. The Act was envisaged as a method of encouraging free trade by freeing the sale of beer from a restrictive licensing system. There was also a view that beer was a more wholesome drink than spirits and should be encouraged. The impact was immediate and produced a free-for-all. In the first year of the new regime over 31,000 licences were issued in England and Wales and within four years there were more than 45,000 beer houses. In Norwich, a local newspaper reported that 'many applications had been made for licences' and that the price of beer had been reduced by about two pence a quart. Within a decade the city had at least 53 beer houses amongst its 600 drinking places. By the time the system was changed in 1869, when the licensing system was tightened up and beer houses were required to apply to the Licensing Magistrates, there were still 40,000 across the country. The major impact of the Beer Act was not on the common brewers but more on the brewing

publicans who lost trade and in some cases were forced to close.

As the city's population grew during the nineteenth century so did the number of public houses and Norwich became known for having more pubs per head of population than anywhere else. In 1801 there was one pub for every 121 of the population and although this declined to one for every 175 by 1896, it remained the highest in the country. On average, during the period from 1867 to 1893 there were at least 530 licenced premises in the city. Public houses were also used by thousands of people as social centres and the focus of sporting activities such as cycling clubs and boxing. They were also used, until the law was changed, as committee rooms at election times, and on occasion as the venue of coroners' inquests.

> **A directory for 1869 listed 474 public houses in Norwich, although it seems likely that the city had more than 600.**

DRUNKENNESS AND PROSTITUTION

The large number of public houses in Norwich was a major cause of concern – the age-old problem of taverns and public houses being associated with drunkenness, disorder and prostitution. There was much public disquiet about pubs being used for prostitution and representations were made regularly to the licensing authorities. The trade was also being faced with an increasingly active and influential temperance movement from the 1840s. In 1850 Jeremiah Colman presented a petition to the Norwich Town Council requesting that no new licences be granted because of 'the riot and debauchery that accompanied drinking'. The petition was refused on the casting vote of the Mayor. The following year there was another petition claiming that Norwich had more public houses than many other towns; that most crime was carried out by people who had been drinking, and requesting that the Magistrates refuse all further licences. The petition was ignored after several of the Magistrates made derogatory comments about it.

The issues of public houses being used as brothels received wide attention in 1853 when John Dunne, the chief officer of the Norwich police, in evidence to a Parliamentary Select Committee, asserted that 200 of the pubs and beerhouses in the city were notorious brothels. He added that of the 670 beer houses and pubs in Norwich, many were run by returned convicts or convicted felons and used for the receiving of stolen goods. His opinion was that because several brewers sat on the Watch Committee no action was taken to deal with the problem. This drew indignant denials from the Norwich authorities but there is little doubt that the allegations had substance. It seems that very few licences were refused by the Licensing Magistrates because complaints about disorderly houses made by the police went first to the Watch Committee who dismissed those they considered 'childish'. No record was kept of their deliberations or of who attended the meetings. The inference was that the brewers were complicit in allowing their pubs to be used for prostitution and then used their influence on the Watch Committee and the Licensing Magistrates to prevent any complaints being considered. It was noticeable in reports of the Licensing Magistrates meeting held in September of 1853 that although several pubs owned by Steward & Patteson and Peter Seaman were mentioned as being disorderly houses, it was only the licencees of independent public houses who had their licences refused, such as Mrs Bowen of The Grapes in Dove Lane which the police reported had been open until 2 or 3 a.m. with the company 'consisting chiefly of girls of the town'. This was no isolated case and the brewers were clearly using their position as Magistrates and Town Councillors to protect their business interests.

The temperance movement was more difficult for the brewers to deal with. It had significant public sympathy and its supporters included some of the more influential people in Norwich. One such was Samuel Jarrold who had been prominent in the movement since arriving in the city. He and his colleagues campaigned hard to highlight not only the damage done by alcohol – ill health, family break-up and crime – but also the advantages of abstinence and how money spent on alcohol could be more wisely spent on food, housing and other benefits. They arranged well-attended public meetings and Samuel used his own money to buy the Victoria Hall in St Andrews Street as a venue for temperance meetings. He also paid for an organiser to visit people in their homes to convince them to sign the temperance pledge. Their campaigning was accompanied by the distribution of thousands of leaflets, such as the Norwich Tracts – homilies on the dangers of drink and the benefits of abstinence. They were strongly supported by many of the non-conformist churches in the city.

EXPANDING BEYOND NORWICH

By the mid-nineteenth century the large Norwich breweries were expanding beyond the city – purchasing smaller rural breweries across Norfolk and Suffolk along with their tied houses – pubs that were legally committed to buy their beer from a particular brewery. An unintended side-effect of the tied-house system was that a significant number of historic buildings survived because they were in use as public houses. Many of the tied houses were also owned by the breweries – or in many cases by the individual partners in the business. In 1845, Steward & Pattesson had 184 tied houses in Norwich, Bullard 35, John Young 71, Richard Crawshay 21, Morgans 60 and Charles Weston 32. The remaining 90 public houses were either free houses or brewed and sold their own beer. This expansion continued – by 1866 Morgans owned 178 public houses in all.

By 1895 Bullards had 441, and the city's largest brewer, Steward & Patteson, owned 489. In June 1864, the number of major brewers was reduced from five to four following the death of Charles Weston. His brewery, public houses and equipment were auctioned. The brewery and 40 pubs were bought by Youngs, Crawshay & Youngs for £15,300. This left the city with the four large brewers who would dominate the brewing trade for the next century.

To supply their ever increasing number of pubs, the Norwich brewers were producing increasing amounts of beer. In 1869 it was estimated the city's breweries were providing about 230,000 barrels a year, with Steward & Patteson brewing just under half of the total. By this time there were around 118,000 licenced premises in England and Wales. A directory for that year listed 474 public houses in Norwich, although it seems likely that the city had more than 600. Many would have been beerhouses or small back street drinking places. This number would later decline substantially due to a number of factors. The most important was a growing consensus that there were too many pubs and

that many were places of drunkenness, and in some cases dens of vice and criminality. Some magistrates – especially those with temperance views – felt they should use their position to reduce the numbers.

Whilst the brewers became wealthy and an integral part of the city's social, political and business establishment, things were not quite so rosy for their employees. Although large-scale brewing required major capital for investment in plant and for the purchase of public houses, it didn't need a large labour force. In 1879 Steward & Patteson employed only 114 staff at their Pockthorpe brewery. Although some staff were highly skilled, wages were generally low – the average at Pockthorpe in 1896 was only slightly above the average agricultural wage. Despite this, brewery jobs were valued as some brewers provided additional benefits such as modest pensions and housing for their retired workers, whilst others like Bullard & Son had a long tradition of providing annual outings for staff and their wives to Cromer, Great Yarmouth or the Crystal Palace.

Opposite: Steward and Patteson's Pockthorpe offices.
Left: Youngs, Crawshay and Youngs' King Street brewery.

LAGER AND BOTTLES

Until about 1880 most beer had been supplied in barrels. In Norfolk, the main beer was traditionally a strong mild although 'London Porter' – a darker hopped beer – had been brewed in Norwich since the 1840s. After 1880, European-style lager beers began to be imported into Britain and in the 1890s bottled beer became increasingly popular. In 1896 Bullards alone sold 84,000 bottles – vindicating their decision the previous year to begin producing it. These new beers were accompanied by major investment as the Norwich brewers sought to remain competitive. Steward & Patteson introduced cask washing machines in 1898 (previously it had been done by hand), installed a new fermenting room and in 1907 built a new pneumatic maltings.

DOMINATION

Toward the end of the nineteenth century brewing in Norwich was dominated by four large firms – Bullard & Sons, Morgans & Company, Youngs, Crawshay & Youngs, and Steward & Patteson, the largest. All were partnerships, usually composed of a small group linked by family ties. They controlled the majority of the public houses in Norwich and the surrounding area. In 1914 within the city itself Bullards owned 133, Steward & Patteson 128, Youngs,

Crawshay & Youngs, 88, whilst Morgans owned 74. The only interloper was Great Yarmouth-based Lacons which had 32 pubs. The Norwich brewers were large businesses both in their own right and nationally. They dominated the supply of beer locally – much more so than breweries in other parts of the country – whilst Steward & Patteson was one of the largest brewers outside London. The more ambitious looked further afield for business. Harry Bullard was a prominent member of one of the English syndicates which invested heavily in American breweries in the 1890s, and was the chairman of a major South African brewery.

The Norwich brewers were always endeavouring to improve their tied-house estates by disposing of houses which sold little beer and acquiring new, more profitable ones. They were assisted in this by the 1904 Licensing Act which permitted public house licences to be surrendered in return for compensation. This worked to the brewer's advantage as it enabled them to close some of their more run down and unprofitable pubs and be paid for doing so.

Above, left to right: A view of the offices at Steward and Patteson's Pockthorpe brewery in 1974; Morgan's delivery fleet lined up for inspection in the 1940s.

Steward & Patteson closed 20 pubs in Norwich during the decade following the Act and received over £23,000 in compensation. Most of the Norwich pubs that were closed were selling less than 100 barrels of beer a year.

Facing the need to remain competitive, to raise money for investment and to protect the partners from any future liabilities, the big four, like many other businesses at this time, changed their legal status by assuming limited liability. This was an important step as partners in a business did not have the protection afforded by limited liability. The first to do so was Morgans, which became a private company in 1887. Within a decade the others had followed suit. They all remained family controlled, usually the ordinary shares were retained by the former partners and the preference shares or debentures were offered for sale. These were quickly snapped up by both professional investors and local people who recognised that brewing was profitable and likely to pay regular dividends.

HARD TIMES

The First World War put a brake on the continued growth and prosperity of the brewing industry. Taxation on beer increased, there were restrictions of the supply of raw materials and consumption of beer declined. By 1918 production of beer had dropped by 25% on pre-war levels and did not recover. There were now alternatives to public houses as places of recreation with the growth of the wireless, the cinema and mass spectator sports such as professional football for people to spend their time and money on.

The Norwich brewers responded by a process of rationalisation – smaller breweries were bought. Steward & Patteson bought Pearses of East Dereham in 1922 and the long established family firm of Bagges of Kings Lynn in 1929. The brewery was usually closed and its tied houses supplied from Norwich. There was further investment in plant, and the use of motor vehicles enabled pubs further away

from Norwich to be supplied. The purchase of other breweries and new investment was paid for by the sale of shares – this time to the general public as the Norwich brewers became public companies listed on the Stock Exchange. Steward & Patteson went public in 1936 and although still largely controlled by the same families as before, their control was diluted – a step which would ultimately lead to the demise of the brewing industry in Norwich.

The inter-war period saw the growth of council housing in Norwich as the City Council cleared away some of the city centre slums and resettled people on new estates on the city's outskirts. The brewers went with them, building large comfortable pubs – such as the King's Arms on Mile Cross Road or the Woodcock on the Catton Grove estate – to serve the new communities. Many older and less profitable pubs in the city were closed and demolished.

In contrast to the First, the Second World War was good for the brewers. Output increased to serve a workforce that was in full employment, especially in East Anglia with its many rural pubs serving agricultural workers, and profits were healthy. Although the cost of raw materials and the duty on beer increased, the brewers compensated by cutting their costs and reducing the strength of their beer.

The post-war period saw further takeovers – Steward & Patteson took over Soames of Spalding and its 240 pubs in 1949, and diversified into the manufacture of soft drinks, mineral water and the sale of wines and spirits. Superficially, all was well – the Norwich brewers provided beer to hundreds of tied pubs in Norfolk, Suffolk, Essex, Cambridgeshire and Lincolnshire, and had no challengers. In 1955 Steward & Patteson alone owned 842 pubs and acquired a further 400 when taking over Ely-based East Anglian Breweries in 1957. However, many of the pubs in rural areas, and some in Norwich, sold few barrels of beer each week and were sustained for their social value to the local community, despite not being profitable.

TAKEOVER AND CLOSURE

To the outside observer the Norwich brewing industry was strong and prosperous. The British Association in 1961 reported that the three remaining city brewers – Steward & Patteson, Bullards, and Morgans – employed over 900 people between them and supplied 2,500 licenced premises across Norfolk, Suffolk, Cambridgeshire and Lincolnshire but the founding families were no longer the major shareholders and by the late 1950s no longer held controlling interests. This left them vulnerable to takeover. The first to go were the two smaller Norwich brewers – Morgans, and Youngs, Crawshay & Youngs. In 1958 Youngs was taken over by Bullards, who had held shares in the business for over 15 years. Young's Crown Brewery in King Street was closed: it later became the Wensum Lodge adult education centre. Three years later it was the turn of Morgans. The firm was bought jointly by Steward & Patteson and Bullards. The large modern Morgan's brewery in King Street, rebuilt following war damage, was sold to Watney Mann who began brewing beer in Norwich.

Watneys then began buying shares in both Steward & Patteson and Bullards. There was no resistance from the major shareholders and in 1963 both companies became part of the Watney empire. Despite public announcements that both Bullard's Anchor brewery and Steward & Patteson's Pockthorpe site would be kept open, both were closed within a few years. The Anchor brewery closed in September 1968 and Pockthorpe a few months later. Production was maintained by Watney at the former Morgan's brewery in King Street where Norwich Mild and

Norwich Bitter were produced, and it was even refurbished in 1973, but closed in the summer of 1985 and later demolished.

The closure of local breweries and the disappearance of long established Norwich beers provoked a backlash and stimulated the growth of the Campaign For Real Ale (CAMRA) in the 1970s encouraging an interest in the brewing and drinking of 'real' ales. A consequence was the re-emergence of brewing in Norfolk, albeit on a small scale, and there are now a number of well-established local breweries. Another manifestation of the city's love of beer is the annual Norwich Beer Festival which has been a popular part of the social calendar since 1977 and attracts thousands of beer drinkers to St Andrew's Hall each autumn.

There are still visible reminders of the city's brewing industry – the crown gatepost and old brewery buildings at Wensum Lodge, the converted fermentation block of the Anchor brewery in Westwick Street, and the former Steward & Patteson's offices at the junction of Silver Road and Barrack Street, but there is no longer the smell of malting barley as you walk along King Street. It is interesting to speculate whether the Norwich brewers could have maintained their independence and continued brewing as did Greene King at Bury St Edmunds and Adnams at Southwold but it seems that the directors had no confidence in a future for locally owned breweries.

Below, left to right: The former Watney's bottling store in King Street prior to demolition; Watney's King Street brewery in 1964.

Opposite: Youngs, Crawshay & Youngs' Crown Brewery, now Wensum Lodge.

BULLARD AND SONS

Bullard and Sons may not have been the largest brewers in nineteenth-century Norwich but they were the most efficient and innovative, thanks to the foresight and determination of Richard Bullard, the founder of the business, and his son Harry who succeeded him.

Born in Norwich in 1808, Richard Bullard appears to have started out at premises in Lower Goat Lane where he brewed and sold beer but by 1838 had moved to St Miles Bridge (on Coslany Street) where he described himself as a 'Brewer, Maltster and Liquor Merchant'. At what became known as the Anchor Brewery, Bullards would brew beer for over a century, and the anchor would become the company's trademark. Beer was brewed for the wholesale and retail trade and the business advertised that it also sold 'Truman's Fine London Brown Stout and Porter, in bottles and on draught'. By the following year he and his partner James Watts were trading as brewers and maltsters, and importers of foreign wines and spirits. The pair also sold corn and had a flourishing trade supplying coal for poor relief to parishes outside Norwich.

Opposite: The Anchor brewery. Right: Richard Bullard, founder of Bullard and Sons.

STEAM POWER

The partnership did not last long, being dissolved in June 1847 when Bullard took sole control and concentrated on brewing. It was a competitive business – a Norwich directory of the period lists 17 other brewers. However, with the help of John Briggs, who was married to his sister-in-law, and that of his son-in-law John Boyce, he expanded the brewery, buying adjoining properties in 1850, and installing new equipment. In 1856 steam power was introduced when a 'Cornish' boiler was ordered and an eight horsepower engine supplied by a local engineer. Further boilers followed and as beer sales increased larger fermentation tanks were bought. In 1864 refrigerators were introduced to assist the brewing process and provide cold storage.

Richard Bullard lived initially in a house at the Anchor brewery where six of his ten children were born, but later moved to Poringland. He subsequently returned to Norwich to live on St Giles Street (the house stood on the site of the current Masonic Hall) and spent the last few years of his life at Earlham Lodge. Of his six sons, four played a part in the business, although three of them, Dick, Arthur and Charley, died relatively young. For a period he took an active part in local politics, serving as a Councillor for the ward where his brewery was located. Prior to his death in February 1864, he became reclusive – an obituary described him as becoming 'hypochondriacal, and removed from the society of his friends, to bury himself in the solitude of Earlham'. He left an estate valued at just under £50,000.

Left: Harry Bullard, the driving force behind the success of Bullard and Son, pictured in 1880. Opposite, top to bottom: Coopers at the Anchor brewery in 1913; The former fermentation house as it is today.

HARRY BULLARD

Harry Bullard succeeded to the business at his father's death although it is almost certain he was playing a prominent part before. During the next 40 years Harry Bullard, with the support of his business partners – initially John Briggs, and later John Boyce – developed and expanded the business, investing in new equipment to take advantage of developments in brewing technique.

The business became known as Bullard and Sons, being managed by Harry Bullard, his brother Charley, Briggs and Boyce. At Briggs' death in 1874, Charley and Frederick Bullard joined Harry as partners and when Charley died the following year he was replaced by Boyce. Born in East Dereham, Boyce was the son of a watchmaker and had joined Bullards shortly after marrying Harry Bullard's sister Emma in 1853. He was to prove a great asset. He rarely took a holiday and devoted enormous energy

to the business. His obituary commented that 'its success [was] in part due to his energy and business capacity'. The three partners were to manage the business until it became a limited liability company in 1894.

Bullards continued to expand. To meet the demand for additional power, larger steam engines were bought, a cask washing machine was installed in 1867 and a year later the chimney, which would become a city landmark, was built. Work began in March 1868 with Harry Bullard laying the first brick and by July the 120-foot-high chimney was complete. Throughout the next 20 years further improvements were made – the boilers were replaced, hoists to move the beer barrels from floor to floor were installed, the offices rebuilt, and in 1881 an artesian well 165 feet deep was bored to provide a supply of clean water for brewing.

By 1877 the Anchor brewery was a major industrial complex that dominated Westwick Street, employing 300 men and operating every day of the year, including Sundays, producing 140,000 barrels annually. A contemporary press report described it as covering 'an area of some four or five acres, that has daily three huge coppers containing between two and three hundred barrels each, with two great mashing tuns mashing each 70 quarters'. It was one of the most modern breweries in Norwich.

ACQUISITIONS

The expansion was assisted by the acquisition of other breweries and maltings – as in 1878 when Harry Bullard and Boyce bought the maltings at Reepham formerly owned by Bircham and Sons. They recognised the importance of securing outlets for their beer and, like the other Norwich brewers, steadily acquired public houses which sold only Bullard's beer.

Owning 67 pubs in 1867, within 25 years Bullards had 118, of which 94 were in Norwich. With the exception of Steward & Patteson, Bullards owned more pubs than any other Norwich brewer.

The firm was careful in its selection of pubs and choice of landlords. They wanted to provide security of tenure and to establish a long-term relationship between the landlord and brewer and a steady income for the brewery. It has been calculated that for the period from 1843 to 1867 the licencees in about two thirds of Bullard pubs served for an average of seventeen years. In many instances being a licencee in a Bullard pub became a family tradition – being passed from father to son.

> With the exception of Steward & Patteson, Bullards owned more pubs than any other Norwich brewer.

Bullard pubs also had a reputation for being well managed, with few disturbances involving the police. In contrast, their Norwich rivals, Morgans, although having fewer pubs in the city, had a higher turnover of landlords and owned many more pubs viewed as places where disorder was frequent.

Bullards also provided social treats for their staff and for a number of years organised a summer excursion. The brewery was closed and all the staff, along with their wives or girlfriends, enjoyed themselves at the company's expense. The first excursion, in August 1877, was to Whitlingham.

The staff were conveyed there in two barges, suitably fitted out and decorated, towed by the steamer Alexandra. Two large marquees had been set up by the ruined church on the south bank where a hearty lunch was followed by speeches from Harry Bullard and John Boyce, and a vote of thanks from three of the company's longest serving workers. The afternoon was spent relaxing or playing games before tea was served. At 8 p.m. the whole party was taken back to Foundry Bridge. Later excursions were more ambitious – the following year saw a trip to the Crystal Palace, and in 1880 a special train took 650 to the Alexandra Palace, stopping at Cambridge for refreshments, before returning to Norwich by 11 p.m.

Left:
The chimney at the Anchor brewery, before its demolition in 1982. Opposite, top to bottom: The engineer's shop; Fermenting tuns at the Anchor brewery in the early twentieth century.

MINERAL WATER

The firm was prompt in responding to new opportunities. Identifying a public demand for soft drinks, Bullards built a mineral water plant in Lower Westwick Street adjacent to the brewery in 1897. Provided with electricity from a dynamo supplied by Laurence Scott, the plant produced various carbonated sweet drinks and ginger beer and had capacity to turn out up to 17,000 bottles a day.

In the spring of 1894 the business became a private limited liability company known as Bullard & Sons Ltd with a capital of £650,000. At the time it controlled 441 pubs, owning the freeholds of 280 of them. The existing partners retained control by taking up the whole of the preference and ordinary shares, but £360,000 worth of mortgage debenture stock at 4% was offered to the public. This was massively oversubscribed – a recognition that Bullards was a company likely to make money for its shareholders. The new company had three directors, Harry Bullard, John Boyce, and George Coller, a wealthy Norwich coal merchant who also had extensive interests in malting.

By the end of the nineteenth century Bullard's Anchor brewery was a successful modern business utilising the most up-to-date brewing techniques. From the point where the malt arrived from the firm's maltings across Norwich, the process of brewing beer was semi-automated with malt being converted to wort before being boiled, cooled and fermented in the 18 fermenting tuns. The beer was then racked and put in barrels before being stored in the refrigerated cellars. There was also a cleansing section where casks were cleaned and inspected prior to being filled with beer. The returned empty beer bottles were also cleaned, being washed at the rate of 1,400 per hour before being refilled. Supplying bottled beer had become an important part of the company's trade. The brewery also had its own cooperage which repaired barrels and made delivery drays and other carts. There were stables for up to 80 horses, together with a blacksmith's shop and harness room.

DEATH OF HARRY BULLARD

Bullards was supplying pubs across Norfolk, of which over 100 were in Norwich, and making money for its shareholders. However it was to suffer two major blows in a short space of time with the loss of John Boyce and Harry Bullard. Boyce died suddenly in August 1900. He had been associated with the firm for over 40 years and his energy and business ability had been instrumental in its success. His sympathetic manner made him popular with the workforce. But perhaps the bigger blow was the death of Harry Bullard who died at 8.40 on the morning of Saturday 26th December 1903 at his Hellesdon House home. In poor health for some time, he had been suffering from diabetes which appears to have been exacerbated by being knocked down by a cab

in London in May 1902. His death generated massive coverage in the local press which chronicled his accomplishments in detail. It also recorded his human qualities, describing him as 'rough and ready in many ways, utterly incapable of the affectations and pretences of conventional politeness' but also a man with a 'natural instinct of sympathy and kindliness'. He was later to be described as 'probably the best known citizen in all Norwich'.

If anyone could have been said to have been born to be a brewer it was Harry Bullard. He was born at the Anchor brewery in March 1841 and attended Harper's commercial academy in Pottergate along with brothers Dick and Charlie. He also appears to have attended the Grey Friars Priory School in Upper King Street run by William Brooke. After being articled to a London wine merchants he visited Spain and Portugal to study the making and blending of wine before joining his father's business not long before Richard Bullard's death.

Harry followed his father in becoming a member of the Norwich Town Council for the Second ward where he missed no opportunity to promote the benefits of beer. At a meeting of the Norfolk and Norwich Victuallers he commended the conduct of the city's licencees,

pointing out that not one had had their licence revoked at the most recent licensing session. He also claimed that licenced victuallers promoted the moral and social improvement of the people of Norwich. Initially a Liberal, he quickly joined the Conservatives saying 'his party having abandoned their original principles, he found himself constrained to join the Conservative ranks, whose policy he deemed to be the safer for the interests of the country'.

THE GOOD CITIZEN

Harry Bullard served as Mayor of Norwich three times but it was during his first term that his energy and determination brought him public acclaim. He had been in office only a few weeks when, in November 1878, the river Wensum overflowed its banks after heavy rainfall. Several of the adjacent parishes were badly flooded. Two men were drowned and the Anchor brewery was inundated. Bullard initiated relief efforts – coffee, tea and bread were provided in the schools, and the governor's house at the former City Gaol was heated and made available for those left homeless to sleep in. He also used his brewery wagons to distribute food. After the floods subsided, Bullard initiated a public subscription which raised over £5,000 to supply food, coal and coke, and provide new furniture for those affected.

At the end of his second term as Mayor in the autumn of 1880, Bullard was a well-known and popular figure. He was asked to stand as the Conservative candidate in that year's general election but refused. Five years later he was again asked and this time agreed. At the election held on 25th November he came top of the poll and was elected along with the Liberal candidate Jeremiah Colman – Norwich then being a single Parliamentary constituency which returned two Members of Parliament. But Bullard was prevented from taking his seat in the House of Commons as a petition alleging bribery, treating (the provision of food and drink to voters), and exercising undue influence, was lodged by his political opponents. After a lengthy trial at The Guildhall, Bullard was unseated.

Opposite: A reminder of the site's former use.

Below: Bullard directors in 1923.

He seems to have been unfortunate as he was personally exonerated but one of his supporters, a man named Walter Banham, was found to have given money to a voter as an inducement to vote for Bullard. Bullard was also prohibited from being a Parliamentary candidate for seven years.

Once the ban expired Bullard was again nominated as a Conservative candidate and in 1895 was elected along with Sir Samuel Hoare – giving Norwich two Conservative MPs for the first time since 1837. This time there was no petition and Bullard took his place in the House of Commons. He was returned unopposed at the following general election and was an MP at the time of his death.

During the last decade of his life, Harry Bullard expanded his interests beyond Norwich, becoming heavily involved in brewing in the United States. From 1885 he was a regular visitor to the US, part of one of the so-called 'English syndicates' which raised large amounts of capital in London to purchase American breweries. Bullard was particularly involved in the Milwaukee and Chicago Brewery Company which for a period generated large profits for its investors. He was also a regular visitor to South Africa where he oversaw substantial investment in Ohlssons Cape Breweries from 1890 onwards. Profits were considerable – rising from £93,000 in 1900 to £167,000 within two years.

Above: Filling the barrels in the 1960s.

Opposite: The former offices at the Anchor brewery.

Bullard's death and that of John Boyce left a huge gap in experience and knowledge but it was quickly filled. Donald Gaul, the former company secretary, was appointed to the board of directors where he was joined by Harry's son Edward, and his nephew Ernest, whilst Gerald, another of Harry's sons, managed the mineral water plant. It was still a family business and was to remain so for a further 60 years. Ernest had joined the firm as a boy and stayed with Bullards for the rest of his working life, becoming a director in 1918. He died in 1946.

FURTHER ACQUISITIONS

The business continued to thrive and expand – it remained one of the four large brewing firms that dominated the trade across East Anglia. In 1924 it took over Bidwells, followed by Hogge and Sepping in King's Lynn four years later. Bidwells was a family-owned brewers which owned over 100 pubs and hotels in south Norfolk, Suffolk and Cambridgeshire supplied from their Thetford brewery.

By 1937 Bullards controlled about 530 tied houses across the region and its anchor trademark and 'jolly landlord' figure were familiar to thousands of pub goers. The Second World War brought damage to maltings near the Anchor brewery but little other interruption.

The 1950s was a successful decade for the firm. It was making six figure profits most years and paying double digit dividends to shareholders – the highest being 22.5% in 1952, the lowest 12% in 1954 and again the following year. At that time Bullards was positive about the future. The brewery capacity was expanded in 1957 and the bottling store extended. Gerald Bullard had become Chairman in 1951 – the fourth generation of the family to have run the firm. He had joined in 1937 after learning the rudiments of brewing at the Birmingham School of Brewing and would remain in control until the takeover by Watneys some 12 years later. In his comments on the annual report for 1960 he 'anticipated favourable trading' and reported that poorly performing pubs had been sold and the company had set aside over £62,000 to invest in improvements – a three-fold increase on the previous year.

But storms were on the horizon. By the late 1950s the brewing industry was consolidating, smaller provincial breweries were being taken over and closed as larger brewers looked for additional outlets for their beer. Bullards joined in, buying their Norwich rivals Youngs, Crawshay and Youngs in 1958. This gave them additional pubs plus Young's King Street brewery which they closed. Three years later Bullards joined forces with Steward & Patteson to buy Morgans, the other remaining Norwich brewery. Morgan's King Street brewery was sold to Watney Mann and their 400 pubs were divided between the new owners. Gerald Bullard later said that he and John Morse, the chairman of Steward & Patteson, had cut cards to decide who should have first pick of the Morgan's pubs.

By the time the takeover was complete Bullards owned almost 900 pubs across the region. But, despite their success, the firm's independence was to be shortlived as in 1963 Watney Mann began buying shares in the business and was obliged by the takeover code to make it public and offer to purchase all the shares. Watneys offered one of their ordinary shares plus 12 shillings for every two Bullard shares. This valued the Bullard shares at 19 shillings each – not considered a good price but one that was accepted by the majority of the shareholders and Bullards consequently changed hands. It was evident that what Watneys wanted was the Bullard pubs. Their chairman commented the following year that Bullard's pubs were 'well suited to provide the extra capacity we require and a more economical distribution of our products'. Ironically, shortly after the takeover was announced Bullard's pre-tax profits for the year ending 30th September 1963 showed an increase of 7.5% to some £628,000.

Right: Bullard's trademark anchor overlooking the resident's car park at Anchor Quay.

WATNEYS ARRIVE IN NORWICH

The chairman of Watney Mann (Norwich) commented that 'there will have to be economies made' but 'the merger could be of great advantage to all three companies concerned [Watneys had also taken over Steward & Patteson], to shareholders, employees and to consumers'. Watneys attempted to address public concern over the loss of local beers by reducing the price of some beers at Bullard and Steward & Patteson pubs. Watney's Brown Ale and a pint of Red Barrel were reduced by two pence whilst Red Barrel Export Ale was reduced by a penny halfpenny.

Within four years brewing ceased at the Anchor brewery. For a short period Bullard's beer was brewed at Watney Mann's King Street brewery and brought by tanker to Westwick Street for racking, bottling and dispatch, but in late 1968 the whole site was closed and offered for sale. It stood empty for many years slowly decaying. There were several proposals for re-development including one for a fleamarket and offices.

In June 1982 the chimney was demolished as it would have proved costly to repair and a prospective developer felt the chimney would deter potential house buyers. Fittingly, it was demolished as it was built – brick by brick.

Eventually the Anchor site was re-developed to provide housing – some of the brewery buildings, including the fermentation hall, were retained but much was demolished. A reminder of its former use is the huge anchor retained on the wall overlooking the residents' car park.

Even after almost half a century the decision of Bullard's directors to accept the Watney Mann takeover is difficult to understand. Bullards was a successful and profitable provincial brewery with over 870 pubs, a good record of investment in modernisation and to all appearances a bright future. It was evident why it was attractive to Watney Mann – they were expanding and wanted additional pubs for their beer in an area where they had few.

FOOD MANUFACTURING

The processing or manufacturing of food on a large scale was not a major industry in Norwich until the second half of the nineteenth century. It then grew, flourished, declined and virtually disappeared – all within 100 years.

Traditionally, the preparation and processing of food for sale had been carried out on a small scale by butchers, bakers and millers who served their immediate localities. One of the few exceptions was vinegar which had been brewed on a large scale in Norwich from at least 1762. Vinegar had been used for centuries and was valued for its versatility. The Sumerians of Mesopotamia used it as a cleaner and it later came into widespread use as a preservative and for its medicinal qualities. However, brewing vinegar had its dangers, as Thomas Foyson discovered to his cost in February 1832. Foyson was in partnership as a vinegar brewer in St Georges Street and visited the works by himself one Saturday morning to gauge the amount of vinegar in the vats. It appears that in doing so he overbalanced and fell into the vat where he drowned.

The processed foods which were available were largely those still eaten today including bread, butter, cheese, bacon, meat and fish. These were all produced using well tried and established methods such as salting, curing, curdling, drying, pickling and smoking.

BAKERS

Bread came from the local baker of which Norwich had many. They in turn obtained their flour from the city's millers and flour merchants. In 1783 there were at least six flour merchants trading in the city, some of whom ground the flour at their own mills. There

were mills at Trowse, Lakenham, Costessey, Hellesdon and Sprowston powered by wind or water, but it wasn't until the introduction of roller milling and steam power in the nineteenth century that corn milling could be done on a large scale. Much of the trade in flour and corn took place at public houses near the market on market days.

For hundreds of years meat had been salted to preserve it. Packing the meat in salt reduced the likelihood of bacteria flourishing and kept it edible. Meat treated in this way could last a long time and was particularly valuable on extended sea voyages. It was eventually replaced by frozen and refrigerated foods. Pickling was also used to preserve meat and vegetables which would be soaked in salt water before being rinsed and then stored in vinegar.

Most people obtained their food as and when required from their local supplier or by visiting the market. Every town in Norfolk had a market and Norwich was no different, apart from its size and variety of the goods on sale. It was one of the largest in England and drew traders and customers from a wide area. In the fourteenth century the provision market covered a large area – stretching from Guildhall Hill to St Stephen's Church with a number of specialist areas selling such things as wool, cattle, sheep, leather and metal goods. Wheat was sold beside the church of St Peter Mancroft whilst meat, fish and bread were sold on the upper market, where City Hall now stands. The lower market, by Gentlemans Walk, was reserved for the sale of produce by smallholders from the countryside. By the end of the century Norwich market was said to be 'dominated by stalls providing provisions for the city'.

THE WEALTHY GROCERS

The provision of food became a source of wealth to those that supplied it and some of the city's grocers (traders who sold goods in large quantities) became wealthy men with much of the food stuff they dealt in being delicacies imported from Antwerp. During the reign of Elizabeth I it has been calculated there were about 125 grocers in Norwich at any one time. Some became very wealthy, and prominent in civic life – during this period nearly half of those who held the office of Mayor were grocers by trade. This dominance continued into the seventeenth century when men such as George Cocke who lived at Bacon's House in Colegate, his brother Francis who owned Strangers' Hall, and Adrian Parmenter who was Mayor in 1641 and ran the Excise office from his home on Hog Hill (now Timberhill) became wealthy and powerful though selling groceries. Another wealthy grocer was Augustine Briggs who at his death in 1684 left £9,000 and several properties in Norfolk. His mansion was on what is now Brigg Street – in the centre of the city where he made his money. Grocers during this period not only sold the staples necessary for everyday life such as salt, sugar, dried fruits and spices but also things such as 'horse spice', 'clackchalke', 'nutgalls' and 'wormseed' that are now unfamiliar. Grocers also often acted as tallow merchants, selling the rendered animal fat used for making candles and soap.

The early grocers and the stall holders on the Norwich market were traders in food – buying and selling but not manufacturing. By the late eighteenth century groceries were no longer sold solely at the market and grocer's premises had sprung up across the city. A trade directory of the time lists 37 grocers, some of whom were also wine merchants. Reflecting the continuing importance of the market as the commercial hub of the city's trade, almost half of the grocers were situated there or close by with several having shops on the Upper Market.

FOOD MANUFACTURING

Within a generation, whilst grocers continued to flourish, food manufacturing became a major Norwich industry and firms such as Colman's, Caleys and Coopers became nationally known. Their success was assisted by several factors: the availability of rapid railway transport; a steadily increasing population in Norwich; a supply of cheap labour; and improvements in processing, such as bottling and canning, which enabled their products to have a longer shelf life.

Norwich market was one of the largest in England and drew traders and customers from a wide area.

The period also witnessed the development of pre-packaged and branded goods, such as Brown and Polson's custard powder and Colman's mustard, which were widely advertised and quickly delivered. Local wholesalers, who traditionally bought food in bulk before packaging it for their customers, also began distributing their own branded goods. In Norwich, Copemans sold 'Copeman's Parisien Coffee' and 'Star Baking Powder' whilst W. H. Dakin sold their 'Dak Indo' and 'Gladstone' teas, pre-packed at their Davey Place warehouse.

By the early 1880s there were several major food factories in Norwich. They included Hills and Underwood's Norwich Vinegar Works and Gin Distillery on Prince of Wales Road, Caley's mineral water and chocolate works at Chapelfield, Cooper's confectionery factory at the Albion Mill on King Street, and Colman's Carrow works – the largest of them all.

VINEGAR

Originally located in Queen Street, Hills and Underwood had been built up by Norwich wine merchant David Hills and his partner Joseph Underwood, a London wine merchant and distiller. When Joseph died a wealthy man in 1864, leaving an estate of almost £140,000, his place was taken by his son Frederick who expanded the business substantially. In 1865 a new vinegar works was built off Prince of Wales Road covering a ten-acre site beside the river complete with fermenting facilities, vat and barrel stores, warehousing and a gin distillery. A local press report in 1875 described the works in great detail and explained how the vinegar was made using the most up-to-date scientific methods. It also emphasised most strongly that no sulphuric acid was used in its manufacture! It appears that sulphuric acid was commonly used in the production of cheaper brands and had resulted in cases of poisoning.

In her book *Trades and Industries of Norwich* Joyce Gurney-Read described the process used by Hills and Underwood in making vinegar:

'Making vinegar was very similar to making beer, despite the absence of hops. The fine Norfolk malts were ground to a meal and placed in mash tuns. Here the meal was mixed with hot water and heated to boiling point – producing a wort. The wort was then cooled and placed in fermenting vats, yeast was added and alcohol was produced. This had to be converted to acetic acid; achieved by exposing the liquid to air. At one time this was carried out by vats in open-air vinegar yards but later processes were invented whereby the liquid was slowly trickled over birch twigs, the long exposure to air meaning that acidification could be achieved in 48 hours instead of the lengthy period of three months taken by the open-air method'.

Subsequently the vinegar had to be 'cleaned' and 'clarified' – the resultant fresh malt vinegar being a pale primrose colour. Most customers preferred a darker colour, so caramel was added. This did not alter the taste but merely changed the appearance. Hills and Underwood produced a range of vinegars for different uses, some being sold as salad dressings or as condiments, whilst others were advertised as having medicinal qualities including the ability to cure hiccoughs or ease a sore throat. The firm also made cordials, liqueurs and the 'Celebrated Old Tom Gin'.

Below: Advertisements for Smith's cough medicine and Hills and Underwood's vinegar (1904).

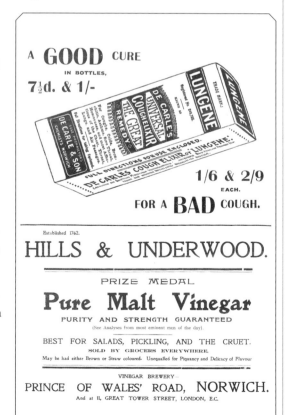

MINERAL WATER AND CHOCOLATE

Albert Jarmen Caley was a chemist who, in 1856, moved from Windsor to Norwich and set himself up in business in London Street, employing two assistants and two boys to help in the shop. It seems likely he was attracted to Norwich by the success of his brother Nathaniel who was a silk merchant with a shop by the market place. Before long Albert had diversified and began making mineral water at premises in nearby Bedford Street. This proved so successful that he abandoned the chemists and began manufacturing mineral water on a large scale. In 1880 he moved to larger premises, buying a former glove cloth weaver's workshop at Chapelfield. By then he was living close by at The Crescent with his family.

It was at Chapelfield that Albert Caley diversified further and began making cocoa and chocolate. Within a few years the firm was also making milk chocolate. At the time Swiss chocolate dominated the English market but, with local supplies of rich milk available from a farm at Whitlingham, Caley decided he could compete and built a new cocoa and chocolate factory near the mineral water factory at Chapelfield. After Albert's death in 1895, his son Edward and nephew Frederick took over the firm which then became known as A. J. Caley and Son. By 1900 Caley's chocolate was being made in large quantities and sold nationally. Around that time the firm diversified even further and began making Christmas crackers, which sold well at home and in France. By the early years of

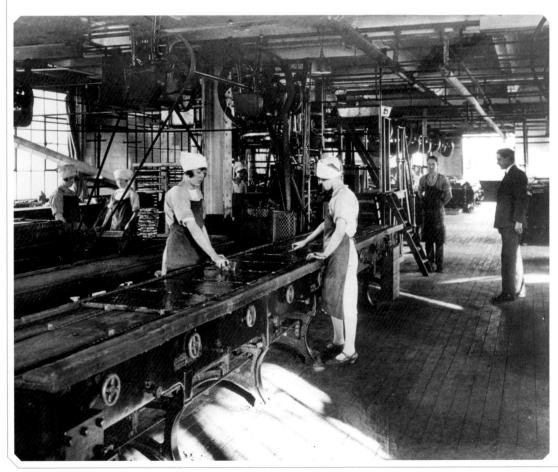

the twentieth century Caleys were employing 700 workers and sending their chocolate and crackers to Canada, South Africa, Australia and India. The period prior to the First World War saw further expansion. In 1907 Caleys opened other mineral water factories, including one in London, and the following year took over the Banham cider making firm of Rout & Co.

CONFECTIONARY

For a period the firm of R. A. Cooper Ltd was the largest firm of confectionary makers in Norwich but the firm's origins were in a Queen Street sweet shop run by George Wilson, whose cakes and ice cream were considered the most delicious in Norwich. When he retired in the 1860s the shop was bought by Robert Aspland Cooper. Born in the Potteries, Cooper never stayed too long in one place and spent time in the United States before coming to Norwich.

He was quick to recognise the increasing demand for cakes and confectionary and set out to make them on a large scale. In 1876 he bought the Albion Mill in King Street, a former yarn factory, and converted it into what was later described as 'a huge confectionary works' where he made crystalised ginger and pineapple, sugar eggs, sugar coated almonds, sugar cigarettes, Turkish delight and jujubes – both sweet and medicinal. Coopers also made over 150 types of biscuits, including the popular 'Norwich Hollow Biscuits', many different types of cake, ranging from half-penny jam tarts to large wedding cakes, and the popular six penny and one shilling Cherry, Currant and Genoa cakes which were sold throughout the country. Jam, marmalade, jellies and baking powder were also turned out in large quantities at the King Street factory – much of which was exported to British colonies and to South America.

WINCARNIS

New firms entered the Norwich food and drink industry in the late nineteenth century including Coleman and Company – the makers of 'Wincarnis' tonic wine, invented by William Juby Coleman, originally a manufacturing chemist in Bury St Edmunds. Coleman had tried his hand at a variety of things and whilst working in London had become involved in the import of meat extracts. He moved to Norwich in the 1870s where he set up in business in St Georges Street and bought a restaurant on Bank Plain. He was an inveterate inventor and his most successful invention was a tonic wine incorporating beef extract which he developed in 1885 and named Wincarnis. Coleman's advertising claimed that Wincarnis was a 'highly scientific combination, principally of Liebigs Extract of Meat, Extract of Malt and Port wine prepared under a carefully considered method, under highly trained supervision, and on true physiological principles' which would provide strength and energy to those of a nervous disposition and cure a range of disabilities by building up the 'nerve forces'.

It was sold by chemists, wine merchants, and by grocers holding a wine licence, at two shillings and sixpence for a small bottle, or four shillings and sixpence for a larger one. Colemans also made 'Cocoa Wine' and 'Coleman's Crown Imperial Invalid Champagne' which they advertised as a 'sound wholesome fruity drink'. The business was later floated as a limited liability company with William Coleman as the managing director and new premises built on Barn Road. He terminated his links to the business in 1911 and retired to live in Brundall where he died in 1918.

Opposite: Making chocolate by hand at Caleys during the 1920s.

ROBT. JOHN READ'S *Superior Roller Flours*

Are Milled from the Choicest Wheats grown and stands unsurpassed for all uses.

City Flour Mills, Norwich.

READ'S SPECIALITIES:
SELF=RAISING FLOUR AND "COUNTRYSIDE" WHEAT MEAL.

They are the Apex of Perfection.

Packed in small linen Bags and sold by all Grocers and Bakers.

A Booklet of Recipes in each Bag.

SMITH AND SONS

Another successful chemist turned food manufacturer was Smith and Sons. Originally a small chemist's shop in Magdalen Street, they expanded into wholesaling and manufacturing under the direction of Joseph de Carle Smith. Upon his retirement his grandson Joseph substantially expanded the business. By 1900 Smith's factories and packing houses dominated the south side of Magdalen Street at Stump Cross. Under their 'Norfolk' brand Smiths manufactured a range of foodstuffs – vinegar, sauces, baking powder, custard and blancmanges that were sold throughout the eastern counties and beyond. As well as supplying chemist's requirements the firm also produced agricultural chemicals including 'Norfolk Farmer's Friend', used for treating wheat.

MILLING

Norwich was a centre for flour milling throughout the nineteenth century and much of the corn grown in Norfolk was traded at the Corn Exchange near the provision market. Amongst the larger millers were Colman's at Carrow, and John Lee Barber at Westwick Street but perhaps the most successful was the firm founded by Robert John Read. He was a miller from Suffolk who had moved to Norwich and bought a flour mill on Westwick Street near the New Mills after a fire destroyed his Beccles mill in 1896. At New Mills he built a successful business producing self-raising flour and Read's 'Countryside' wheat meal. This was in spite of another major setback in 1912 when the new mill was damaged by the flooding which badly affected low lying areas of the city.

Opposite:
Albion Mill in
King Street.

Above: An early
twentieth-century
advertisement
for Read's flour.

CHANGES

By the early twentieth century the food and drink industry was the second largest employer of labour in Norwich behind boot and shoe-making, with Colman's Carrow works alone employing over 2,500 workers. The major firms produced branded foodstuffs that were sold nationally. Packing of food and drink, excluding the breweries, was very labour intensive. One contemporary observer estimated that almost two thirds of the labour in the industry was made up of women, girls and boys. Wages were low but there was little casual labour – what there was being largely confined to seasonal work such as jam boiling and the manufacture of mineral water.

A directory published just before the turn of the century demonstrates the extent of the industry. It listed six mineral waters manufacturers, two mustard manufacturers in addition to Colman's, five vinegar makers, nine biscuit makers, seven confectionary manufacturers and six baking powder manufacturers. There were also the firms that supplied and supported the industry, such as Bagshaws the paper bag manufacturers in Oak Street, and at least four box makers. Most of the factories were within the old city walls, many in the traditional industrial area north of the river or along the major roads into the city such as King Street and St Benedicts Street.

Left: Henry Robertson, one of the directors at R. A. Cooper.

The decline of food manufacturing in Norwich was gradual but seemingly unrelenting as locally owned firms were taken over or production moved elsewhere. The first to go was Hills and Underwood, bought by the London-based vinegar makers Sir Robert Burnett and Company in 1910 following the death of Frederick Underwood in November that year. Production was transferred to Burnett's Vauxhall works in London. The Prince of Wales Road works was closed and subsequently demolished.

By 1890 R. A. Cooper Ltd was under new control, Robert Cooper having left Norwich. He died in London in 1907. By then the business that still carried his name had become a limited company controlled by a trio of Norwich businessmen – Edward Johnson, William Shave and Henry Robertson. Robertson was a house furnisher in partnership with Thomas Colman in Queen Street, Shave was a brush manufacturer and Johnson was a senior bank inspector employed by Barclays (formerly Gurneys). The three were also directors of R. B. Hovell and Co, horse hair cloth manufacturers in Calvert Street. The new directors invested substantially in Coopers, doubling the capacity of the Albion Mill and employing representatives to sell their confectionary abroad, concentrating on the British colonies and South America. The firm survived the war but by the late 1920s Johnson, Shave and Robertson had died and by 1932 the business had closed and the Albion Mill stood empty.

That year it was purchased by R. J. Read, now run by the founder's sons. The firm had been looking for a more suitable site. Access to New Mills by river was not ideal – the number of bridges and its position at the limit of the tidal river restricted the size of ships that could reach it. The Albion Mill was refurbished with new plant installed for its role as a flour mill. Alongside milling flour Reads began producing flaked maize for cattle feed. They also started importing oyster shells for sale to poultry farmers – it provided grit to aid digestion and was a source of calcium for the chickens.

By the 1950s the business was well established and flourishing. The modern automated facilities milled East Anglian wheat to supply flour in bulk to biscuit makers. The firm was also diversifying and looking for partners in what was becoming a very competitive trade dominated by several large companies. In January 1965, Reads bought Mitchell's Dereham bakery and the following month agreed to build a new bakery in Norwich at Whiffler Road in partnership with Rank-Hovis-MacDougall to produce bread and cakes under the 'Country Bake' label. Soon afterwards Reads announced they were merging with two other local millers – the long established Norwich business of C E Woodrow and Stalham Flour Mills – to form Norfolk Flour Millers. It was later renamed Read-Woodrow.

READ-WOODROW TAKEOVER

The new business decided to concentrate on flour milling and the animal feed business was sold to Tuck's of Burston in April 1969. The new business was successful initially. Capacity at King Street was increased to meet the growing demand for flour – by 1973 the production capacity there was four times what it had been when the mill was first taken over in the 1930s, and profits for the year were over £100,000. However the oil crisis and recession of the 1970s badly affected the economy and Read-Woodrow was not exempt. Demand fell, Read-Woodrow was unable to sustain its independence and in September 1986 became part of the Anglia Maltings group. The new business had nearly 500 employees with interests in malting, milling, agricultural trading and road transport in Norfolk, Suffolk and Scotland with a turnover of £60 million and assets worth £18 million. Initially prospects looked rosy. The new owners made a substantial investment in the mill; in January 1987 they announced they were spending £200,000 on a new automated packing line for flour and that there would be 24-hour working to meet demand. However, the economic downturn of the late 1980s hit the firm hard.

By December 1992 demand for the company's flour had dropped and although efforts were made to find a buyer for the business there were no takers. Closure was announced just before Christmas. The following April, 60 workers were made redundant along with the ten drivers who delivered the flour, and so flour milling came to an end at the Albion Mill. It was later converted to provide riverside housing.

> By the early twentieth century the food and drink industry was the second largest employer of labour in Norwich behind boot and shoe-making.

SMITH & SON BOW OUT

Smith and Son remained a family owned firm until 1950 when it was sold to William Martindale Ltd, a London-based chemists' suppliers, ending five generations of family ownership stretching back over 160 years. At the time of the takeover Smiths no longer brewed vinegar or made custard but had reverted to being a wholesale chemist. They employed 70 people at the Magdalen Street site where over 20,000 lines were supplied to chemists' shops throughout East Anglia. The business later passed into the control of Savoury and Moore before closing in 1969. The writing had been on the wall some years earlier when 20 clerical staff out of a workforce of 100 had been made redundant after Savoury and Moore centralised its administration at Brighton. The warehouses were demolished in 1972 but the Magdalen Street frontage opposite St Saviour's Church remains.

WINE IN BOXES

Coleman and Company continued to make Wincarnis and had expanded into the wine trade. By 1968 they employed 250 people in Norwich, had a sales force covering the whole of the UK and employed agents in 60 countries. One third of the firm's turnover came from exports. Colemans pioneered the sale of wine in boxes. The Consumers Association described wine sold in this manner as 'mostly undrinkable' but the public felt otherwise and it became very popular. It was a successful company and an attractive target for a takeover. In October Reckitt and Colman made a bid for Colemans offering cash or shares. The directors recommended acceptance and Colemans passed into new ownership. At the time it was reported that it was the first time during the twentieth century that Colmans had taken over another Norwich business. The new owners gave the customary public assurances that the interest of the staff and employees would be safeguarded but within a few years the Barn Road works had been closed and Colemans was absorbed into Reckitt and Colman Vinters. Although no longer made in Norwich, Wincarnis is still available and remains popular in the West Indies and in parts of Asia.

THE FALL, RISE & FALL OF CALEYS

The Caley family had run the business until Edward retired in July 1918 when it was sold to the African and Eastern Trading Corporation. The new owners rebuilt the site, putting up four new factory buildings at a cost of around £500,000 which included the purchase of new machinery. A further £200,000 was spent during the following decade on further improvements. Despite this investment Caleys chocolate developed a reputation for being of poor quality, shopkeepers became reluctant to stock it, and the firm struggled financially.

In December 1932 the Halifax toffee makers John Mackintosh and Son bought Caleys for £138,000. They considered it a bargain price having convinced the sellers to write off much of the value of the stock, plant and buildings during the negotiations. Under the direction of Eric Mackintosh the existing management was restructured, the plant replaced by modern German chocolate-making machinery and staff numbers reduced. The factory was closed for two months so a new production process could be installed and the number of Caley lines made was reduced from over 1,000 to about 20.

The next few years saw further investment including the installation of air conditioning, Mackintosh and Son recognising that chocolate would keep longer if stored under controlled conditions. Eventually plant capable of coping with nearly a million square feet of production space was installed.

New products were introduced including 'Rolo' in 1937 which was immediately successful with demand outstripping the company's capacity to supply it. Mackintosh decided to concentrate on making chocolate. The mineral water factories in Ipswich and London were sold along with the Banham cider making business, although mineral water was still made at Chapelfield until 1954 when Norwich brewers Morgans took it over. By 1939 the factory was making a major contribution to the local economy – buying 35,000 tons of sugar beet and over two million gallons of milk annually, much of it from Norfolk suppliers.

During April 1942 the Chapelfield factory was badly damaged by bombing causing it to be closed. The staff were laid off and some production transferred to Halifax. Rebuilt after the war, it became the headquarters of Mackintosh and Son and the factory where new lines were made, including 'Caramac' bars. By 1961 the Caley name had disappeared and all chocolate was sold under the Mackintosh label. The company merged with Rowntree's in 1969, and was taken over by Nestlé in 1988.

The sweet smell of chocolate from the Chapelfield factory permeated the city centre, reminding everybody of the city's industrial heritage. So it came as huge shock when in November 1994 Nestlé announced the factory was to close in two years' time with the loss of all 900 jobs. There had been huge investment in the factory by Nestlé and many of its products such as 'Rolo', 'Yorkie' and 'Caramac' sold well. However, Nestlé sales overall were falling and the firm had spare capacity at its four UK factories. They had decided that one was to close and Norwich lost out. Despite an energetic campaign against the closure it went ahead. Chocolate making at Chapelfield ended after 100 years and the site is today a shopping mall. Only Colman's remained of the city's food makers.

Opposite:
Exterior of
Caley's factory
on Chapelfield.

COLMAN'S OF CARROW

In 1890, White's Directory of Norfolk claimed that 'the name of Colman is known from Peru to far Cathay'. An exaggeration, but perhaps an understandable one, bearing in mind the success of the firm in selling its mustard across the world.

The firm was then the largest industrial undertaking in Norwich, employing 2,000 people at its Carrow works which was a self-contained industrial city where flour, starch and washing blue were produced, along with the mustard with which the name of Colman became synonymous. Its products were sold in distinctive tins and packets by grocers throughout Great Britain, Colman's having been quick to realise the benefits of having easily recognisable products.

The contribution of the Colman family was not restricted to manufacturing – several played a prominent part in the political and religious life of Norwich and Norfolk and they proved generous benefactors to the city where they made their money.

MILLING AT STOKE HOLY CROSS

The firm's origins were modest. Jeremiah Colman was a flour miller at Bawburgh before moving to Norwich in 1804, buying a windmill just outside Magdalen Gates. In 1814 he moved again, leasing a mill at Stoke Holy Cross, south of Norwich, where flour and paper had been made. There he became a general miller, milling mustard and other seeds for local farmers, selling the residue as cattle cake. Mustard became the mainstay of the business but the firm was always looking for new opportunities. The production of starch, initially made from wheat, began in 1830. Later Colman began selling washing blue.

Jeremiah's marriage to Ann Theobold produced no children but he adopted his nephew James who became a partner in the business in 1823, which then employed around 30 men. Later, two more of his nephews, Jeremiah and Edward, became the firm's London agents. The Stoke Mill was very much a family business. James Colman did some of the sifting and mixing of the mustard flour whilst his wife Mary and their daughters helped out at busy times by labelling the casks. The working hours were long. Beginning at 6 a.m., there was a 30-minute break for breakfast and a lunch break of an hour, before work finished at six in the evening. But there were compensations; Ann Colman ran a clothing club for employees and the firm put on social events including a Christmas dinner in the granary, the beginning of a long family tradition of providing benefits for their workers.

Stoke Mill was originally driven by wind and water but a steam engine was installed in 1845 to provide a more reliable source of power and a new mustard mill was built. But the location had its limitations as access was not ideal – the nearest railway station was several miles away at Swainsthorpe, there was a limited supply of local labour and there appears to have been difficulties over extending the lease. Jeremiah and James began looking for an alternative.

THE MOVE TO CARROW

In 1850 a decision was made to move into Norwich and a riverside site at Carrow was purchased from the Norfolk Railway Company. It provided space to build and allowed for future expansion. There was also a railway siding into the site, providing a connection to London. Another reason for moving into the city was the availability of labour. The decline in the local textile industry, formerly the city's major employer, had left large numbers needing work. Additional land was acquired alongside the river. The move to Carrow took

The bull's head motif, first used in 1855, was an early example of an easily recognisable brand.

Opposite: Carrow works, undated.

Left: Jeremiah Colman.

place over a 12-year period and the Stoke lease was not finally relinquished until 1862. The new site witnessed a gradual transformation with a new mustard mill being erected in 1854, to be followed by starch and flour mills, engine sheds, boiler houses, granaries and stores.

The responsibility for organising the move to Carrow fell on the shoulders of Jeremiah James Colman, who became the senior partner following the death of his father James in 1854 and that of his grandfather three years earlier. Jeremiah James remained the dominant force in the Norwich branch of the firm until his death in 1898. He took an intense interest in every aspect of the business and lived close to the works at Carrow House where he moved following his marriage to Caroline Cozens-Hardy in 1856.

At Carrow, Colman's made four basic products – flour, mustard, starch and blue – which were initially sold in bulk to wholesalers and grocers. After early experiments with individual packaging whilst at Stoke, Colman's went on to develop a range of distinctive packets for their goods, making them instantly recognisable and attractive to an increasingly affluent public. There was a ready market for flour – it was a necessity for baking bread. Mustard was a luxury item which Colman's skillfully marketed as a necessary condiment for beef. Starch and washing blue were sold as items which helped make life better, by making clothes look cleaner and more attractive.

The firm also utilised the by-products from the Carrow works, producing animal feed cake from the starch residue, and manure from the bran left after the extraction of the mustard. Subsequently the oil extracted from the crushing of the mustard seed was advertised as a remedy for rheumatism. The processing of the residue into cattle cake began in May 1852 but quickly generated complaints from local residents about the smell. When the nuisance continued Colman's was fined by the Norwich Magistrates but managed to get the decision overturned later at the Norwich Sessions court on a point of law.

Below: Die stamping the penny tins at Carrow in 1893.

Opposite: Colman's Carrow works.

STARCH, MUSTARD AND WASHING BLUE

This was but a blip on the expansion of the Carrow works. Within a decade of completing the move from Stoke the works had become a large and complicated manufacturing complex, consuming large amounts of raw materials including rice from India and mustard seed from Lincolnshire, Yorkshire and Holland. There was a substantial labour force of some 1,500 men. Large amounts of water were used in the production processes – so much so that in 1862 the company sank a 1,200-foot deep artesian well on the site. Each week 200 tons of coal were used to power the steam engines and over 250 tons of goods left the works by rail along with 1,500 sacks of flour.

Mustard seed was cleaned before being crushed by passing through rollers, then pulverised by giant pestles. The bran was then separated from the mustard flour which was sieved to produce the required grades. By 1890, Colman's were making six different grades of mustard.

Starch was originally made from wheat which was steeped in water before being ground to produce a thick creamy liquid from which a

starch paste was produced, which was dried and heated at a high temperature. The crust was then scraped off before the starch was heated again to produce the finished product. Around 1849, Colman's began using Indian rice instead, using a caustic soda mixture to break up the cellular structure of the rice before the grinding, heating and final preparation. This speeded up the production of starch and made for a more consistent product.

Washing blue was a mixture of starch and dye, used when washing clothes to disguise the yellowing process of whites in particular. It had originally been made for Colman's by Cricks of Bristol until a mill was built at Carrow in 1862 to produce it. Originally a plant-based indigo dye was used but this was superseded by ultramarine which proved easier to work with during the manufacturing process.

The final stage of production was the packing into the various packets, tins, boxes, cases and kegs. These were all made on site as were the wrapping paper and labels. Packing was the most labour intensive part of the process, being carried out by an army of semi-skilled and unskilled women and children, overseen by a nucleus of supervisors. In Norwich,

Colman's was considered to be a good employer, although for most of the workforce there was little security of employment. The boys had to leave when they reached the age of 18 and the girls when they married. However, wages were above the average for the area, there was no casual labour at Carrow and the firm provided a number of welfare benefits. This made Colman's an attractive place of employment in a city where wages were generally low, kept down by the sustained pool of labour supplied by large-scale immigration from the surrounding rural area and lack of competing employment. By 1905 some 2,500 people were employed at the 32-acre Carrow works.

STEAM POWER

From the beginning, the business was ambitious and progressive, always striving to become more efficient and productive. At the Stoke Mill steam power was introduced, and Colman's was quick to utilise the railways for transporting its goods even before the move to Carrow. New products were introduced including corn flour and self-raising flour. In the twentieth century, Colman's became known for its soft drinks, instant mashed potato, baby foods, casserole mixes and sauces, whilst continuing to manufacture mustard, both dried and ready mixed.

Much effort went into developing the distribution and marketing of Colman's products. The London agency, established in 1829 to sell the company's products at home and abroad, became increasingly important and new offices were built in Cannon Street to house it. Colman's was quick to spot the possibilities of the export trade – building on the work done in 1840 when the 22-year-old Jonathan Copeman was sent to Canada and the United States for six months to sell Colman's mustard and flour and find local agents to stock them. By 1913 the firm was exporting mustard widely and had an agreement with Reckitts of Hull to share profits from their respective South American businesses.

PROMOTION

By extensive promotion Colman's established the public perception that its mustard, starch and blue were of top quality and made by a company with a social conscience. The bull's head motif, first used in 1855, was an early example of an easily recognisable brand. The company's products looked distinctive. Some were available in presentation packs such as mustard pots for use at the table. Colourful shop display boards and enamelled signs kept the name of Colman in the public eye, as did posters such as the 'Mustard Girl' designed for the company by John Hassall. By 1900 the company was also distributing educational wallcharts of animals and flowers to schools, all displaying the Colman name and reinforcing the image in the public mind of a socially aware company.

Opposite:
Scraping starch
ready for packing
at Carrow.

Below: An
advertisement for
Colman's starch
from the 1890s.

Colman's spent heavily on advertising but its products were not glamorous and the firm looked for new ways to attract public attention. One such was the Mustard Club – launched in 1926 after much advance publicity. Reputedly based on the Dickens's Pickwick Club it was a tongue-in-cheek stunt whose directors included Baron de Beef, Lord Bacon and Master Mustard. It proved to be very successful, attracting thousands of requests for badges and leaflets, whilst the company's advertising agents devised a series of adventures for the club which were featured on its publicity material. It ran for seven years at great cost and provided Colman's with a lot of publicity but whether it substantially increased sales is open to question.

SOCIAL WELFARE

The Colmans were Baptists and, influenced by their strong nonconformist Christian faith, the family demonstrated a commitment to their employee's welfare. After moving to Carrow, in October 1857 the Colmans established a school for the children of their employees in an upper room off King Street, run by Maria Cogman the former teacher at Stoke. In that initial year the school had only 22 pupils but grew quickly thereafter. The number had

grown tenfold by 1866 and reached 300 four years after that. Much of the cost was borne by the Colman family. The children's parents made a contribution but the fees of one penny for the first child and a halfpenny for each additional child from the same family were only sufficient to pay for the school prizes.

Later a purpose-built school was erected on Carrow Hill. It was passed to the Norwich School Board in 1900 as the company withdrew from education.

There were other employee benefits. Modestly priced midday meals were introduced in 1868. In the first year 10,000 pints of tea and coffee were sold along with nearly 14,000 dinners. Within three years the amount of refreshments provided had grown sevenfold and the meals fourfold. Later a dispensary was opened close to the main gate where employees could receive medical advice and medication free of charge. The company was one of the first to employ industrial nurses – initially male, but later Phillipa Flowerday became the country's first woman industrial nurse. Much of her work involved visiting female employees in their homes to check on their welfare. Housing for ex-employees was built including Carrow Court off Corton Road in Norwich, and at Trowse.

The leisure needs of the workers were not neglected and for several years the company provided an annual tea and sports day in the grounds of Carrow House. In June 1878 it was attended by almost 6,000 employees and their families when there was 'no stint to the refreshment provided' and where, despite the rain showers, a good day was enjoyed by all. These annual treats were later replaced by the award of a day's paid leave.

Left: Phillipa Flowerday, the UK's first female industrial nurse, pictured in 1872 on left.

Opposite: Jeremiah James Colman.

In many ways, the Colmans were comparable to other nineteenth-century social benefactors such as the chocolate-making Cadbury Brothers at Bournville, and soap makers Lever Brothers with their model village at Port Sunlight. Later developments at Carrow would see a pension scheme for employees and in 1918 a Works Council was set up to provide a forum for discussion by employee and management representatives. That same year the directors agreed to give a week's paid holiday to all employees who had at least a year's service.

CIVIC ACTIVITIES

Besides managing the largest manufacturing business in Norwich, the Colman family took an active part in the civic, religious and political life of the city. They espoused the cause of

> In 1857 the Colmans established a school for the children of their employees, which grew to educate 300 children by 1870.

reform, campaigning against the endemic political corruption in the city. One of the weapons they used was the *Eastern Daily Press*, founded by the first Jeremiah Colman in 1845 as the *Norfolk News*, which became a platform for their Liberal nonconformist views.

Several of the family held civic office – Jeremiah was Mayor of Norwich in 1846-7, Jeremiah James in 1862-3, Russell in 1901-2 whilst Ethel, the daughter of Jeremiah James, became the first woman Lord Mayor in 1923-4. But it was Jeremiah James who was the most prominent. First elected to Norwich City Council in 1859, he served for 12 years before becoming one of the Members of Parliament for the city. He retained his seat in the House of Commons until 1895 and although an infrequent speaker there, he was a person of influence in the Liberal Party. He was a towering figure in late nineteenth-century Norwich, a man of enormous energy who managed to run the city's largest business whilst taking an active part in politics for over 40 years.

The family also bequeathed a physical legacy to the city. In his will Jeremiah James left pictures from his extensive collection to the Castle Museum. Concerned at the poor standard of housing for working people in Norwich, Ethel and Helen Colman paid for the building of Stuart Court in Recorder Road, which opened in 1915 providing 22 flats for working people. The family later donated the James Stuart Garden opposite the court to the city, named in memory of the husband of Laura Colman. In the 1920s the sisters renovated the decayed Suckling Hall in St Andrews Street, built the Stuart Hall next door and presented both to the city. Both continue to be well used as a cinema and restaurant. In 1935 Russell Colman paid for a new wing to the Norfolk and Norwich Hospital but in 1946 came the most generous gesture of all when he donated thousands of prints and pictures to the Norwich Castle Museum and provided the money for two new galleries to display them.

LOSS OF JEREMIAH JAMES

By the autumn of 1898 Colman's was the largest manufacturing business in Norwich, employing over 2,000 at Carrow, and one of the 100 largest companies in the country. It was no longer a partnership, having adopted limited liability in 1896, but remained a family owned business with Jeremiah James at its head. However the business was to suffer a series of blows that would affect its future, the first of which was the death of Jeremiah James at the age of 68, in September 1898 at his home near Lowestoft. It was a shock to the firm and to the city. His funeral was a major event with crowds in mourning lining the streets from the Congregational chapel in Princes Street to the Rosary cemetery as the cortège made its way followed by over 1,200 Colman employees.

His death had been preceded the year before by that of his son Alan, who was only 30 when he died but was already a director of the company and a potential future chairman. Following the death of Jeremiah James, his son-in-law James Stuart took over the management of the business but he was incapacitated by illness in 1909 and died three years later. The business continued to prosper but missed the drive and determination of Jeremiah James.

Much of the expansion that followed was by means of takeovers. In 1901 Colman's took over Orlando Jones and Company of Battersea, a long-established firm of starch makers. Two years later mustard makers Keen Robinson was bought. Keen Robinson also made baby food which was a new line for Colman's but one which it developed into a major part of the business. Later acquisitions included Barring, Wallis and Manners, Rimingtons of Selby and Farrows of Peterborough whose range of canned food was added to the Colman's portfolio.

The nature of the business began to change as the firm adapted to meet shifting consumer demand. Mustard remained a staple product but the manufacture of washing blue ceased in 1952. Starch making finished in 1969, although it was continued by Reckitts, and flour making in 1970. The new products included 'Robinson's Lemon Barley', first made in 1935, to be followed by other soft drinks, the short-lived 'Krusto' pastry mix during the 1930s, and 'Jif' lemons in 1956. 'Pom' instant mashed potato was launched in 1961 to be followed by ready-mixed custard in 1963. The 1970s saw dry sauces introduced as the precursor to a range of casserole mixes and wet sauces in jars.

RECKITT AND COLMAN

The structure of the business was also changing. Since 1913 there had been a joint trading and profit sharing arrangement with Reckitts of Hull in South America through a company named Atlantis. After the First World War the arrangement was extended to cover other overseas markets where the two firms operated. Historically there had been close links between the two companies and there had even been discussions in 1898 about a possible amalgamation but they came to nothing. However, 40 years later, in 1938, Colman's of Norwich and Reckitts merged, with the trading assets of both transferred to a holding company to be called Reckitt and Colman Limited, although both continued to trade under their own names. It appears to have been a largely defensive move to formalise the long-standing alliance as both companies emphasised that 'immediate or spectacular results should not be looked for' and the merger was a way of extending to the home market an arrangement that had been in place overseas for many years.

Opposite: The production line for Robinson's soft drinks.

The 1950s witnessed further expansion at Carrow. A new flour mill was built in 1954, a new soft drinks plant in 1955, and in 1959 the massive office block fronting King Street was erected. Four years later Colman's took the first tentative steps into the computer age by introducing punched cards machines. Further acquisitions included Mellor's Sauces, and George Mason Ltd, the makers of OK Sauce. In 1968 Colemans of Norwich, the makers of Wincarnis, was bought. Sodastream was taken over in 1971 and wine makers Edouard Robinson the year after.

Carrow continued to be the centre of food production. In 1973 the company reinforced its reputation as the mustard maker by opening the Mustard Shop in Norwich's Bridewell Alley. The 1980s and 1990s witnessed an end to expansion by takeover as Reckitt and Colman began to divest itself of non-core businesses. The period also witnessed reductions of the Carrow workforce. Over 300 jobs went in February 1983, although it still left a workforce of 2,000.

The wine business was sold in 1988 and production finished at the former Wincarnis premises at Barn Road. The baby food business was sold to Cow and Gate in 1994 and the following year came the sale of the Carrow-based food division to Unilever as Reckitts concentrated on household cleaning products.

Under the management of Unilever, Carrow works continues to make sauces, casserole mixes and mustard. Mustard is still sold with the distinctive yellow and red labels and bull's head logo, continuing over two centuries of mustard making by Colman's. The Colman's Mustard Shop and Museum, operated by Norwich HEART since 1999, in the historic Royal Arcade continues to remind visitors of an important part of the city's heritage and its history of manufacturing.

Below: Colman's Mustard Shop & Museum in the Royal Arcade today.

ENGINEERING

In the mid-twentieth century, engineering was a major industry in Norwich. It employed over 5,000 people – only clothing, footwear, food and drink employed more. The city was home to three large firms each prominent in their field, and many smaller ones. The future seemed secure – presaged in November 1964 by the arrival of a major new industry when Diamond H Controls opened a factory on Vulcan Road North to make electrical switch gear. Yet, within two decades the industry had been decimated by takeovers and closures.

The city's engineering industry had its origins in the iron founders and ironmongers who served the needs of Norfolk's farmers and made pots, pans and grates for domestic customers. From such modest beginnings several innovative businesses evolved which developed products made in Norwich that were sold across the world – including wire netting, prefabricated buildings, and a range of dynamos and electric motors.

CAST IRON

Traditionally, cast iron had been used to make kettles and pots for cooking but by about 1770 it had become feasible to use it for larger items such as load-bearing columns for building work and bridges. An example is the Coslany bridge – dating from 1804 and designed by James Frost, it is the earliest iron bridge in Norwich. Cast iron was also used to make equipment for use in the textile industry – initially spinning frames, but later weaving machines. It would later be used for making railway tracks, domestic utensils, kitchen ranges, heating stoves and sewage and surface water drainage pipes.

Above: Coslany Bridge – the first cast-iron bridge in Norwich.

Where a more malleable material was required as in the manufacture of scientific instruments, clocks and gas fittings, brass was used. Most Norwich iron founders made brass as well as iron castings. Foundry work was dangerous; it involved pouring the hot metal into a mould and allowing it to cool before it was removed from the mould and finished by hand. By the early 1780s there was at least one iron foundry in Norwich – that of Robert Ransome and Company who made stove grates at their foundry near the Whitefriars Bridge and had a shop in the market place. Within a few years three others were listed in a local trade directory.

There appears to have been no clear distinction between iron founders, ironmongers and agricultural implement makers in the early nineteenth century, they all made what their customers asked for – whether it was a Norwich resident wanting a fire grate or a farmer requiring a plough. One of the first successful ironmongers was William Moore, a farmer's son from Wareham in Norfolk, who opened a business in London Street in 1797, close to the junction with Swan Lane. He later went into partnership with John Barnard, trading as Moore and Barnard, ironmongers and stove grate manufacturers.

After Moore's death in 1839 Barnard took Willam Boulton into partnership and expanded into other premises on London Street. By 1864 Barnard had died and Boulton leased a small foundry works on Rose Lane where he manufactured agricultural and horticultural implements, iron gates and fencing and kitchen equipment. The London Street shop was sold and Joseph John Dawson Paul made manager of the new works. Paul would play a crucial role in the development of what would become Boulton and Paul.

BARNARDS

Like Boulton and Paul, Barnards owed its beginnings to ironmongery. Charles Barnard started in business as an ironmonger near the Norwich market place in 1826 but by 1842 had his own workshops in Pottergate making domestic and agricultural ironwork. As the son of a farmer he was conscious of the damage done to crops by rabbits and foxes and thought it could be controlled by suitable fencing. After much experimentation, by 1844 Barnard had managed to weave wire netting using a wooden loom. It would be the foundation of the firm's success for the next 150 years.

Below, left to right: Making wire netting in the 1920s; Wire weavers circa 1910. Opposite: Barnard's Norfolk Iron Works in Coslany Street in the nineteenth century.

NORFOLK IRON WIRE & GALVANIZING WORKS

Two years later he went into partnership with John Bishop who had arrived in Norwich from Bath. In 1859 Charles Barnard's two eldest sons Charles and Godfrey joined their father and the firm became known as Barnard, Bishop and Barnard. It then had some 163 employees, most of whom were employed in the workshop. From Pottergate the business moved to Calvert Street but by 1871 had acquired a riverside site in Coslany Street at what became known as the Norfolk Iron Works. The works contained a blacksmith's shop, several five-storied workshops and a large foundry at the eastern end of the works. About 400 men and boys were employed there making wire netting, fencing, garden chairs, lawn mowers, gates and almost every type of horticultural implement. The works also produced bedsteads, mangles and cooking ranges. Some of its work was more elaborate – in 1862 they made the gates given to the then Prince of Wales by the City of Norwich, as a gift to celebrate his wedding. Designed by Thomas Jeckyll, they took three years to make and were paid for by public subscription. The gates were installed at the royal residence at Sandringham.

At the time Barnard and Boulton were establishing their businesses, the development of the steam engine was providing a new source of motive power. It found many uses – in railway locomotives, for pumping water, providing power for yarn spinning, for milling, and later to drive threshing machines. There was also a need for engineers to build and service them. Some of the Norwich foundries and the implement makers were quick to recognise the possibilities and began producing a range of steam-powered equipment. One was Thomas Smithdale, who by 1850 was in business at St Anne's Foundry in King Street. Within six years he had a workforce of 25, including half a dozen skilled craftsmen, and by the following decade the foundry was capable of

making castings of up to 10 tons. The workshops contained some of the heaviest machinery in Norwich. They advertised that they could supply steam engines from three horsepower up to 100 horsepower and make hydraulic presses, cranes, mills, shaping and drilling machines, along with boilers of all sizes. Smithdale also made pipes, castings and engines for the Gas Light Company and did work for the Great Eastern Railway.

Riches and Watt, engineers and machine makers, were contemporaries of Smithdale, and made condensing engines, vertical cylinder engines and threshing machines at their Dukes Palace Iron Works. The firm also made mills for grinding corn and linseed, pumping machinery and agricultural machinery such as cultivators and field rollers.

JOHN HOLMES

One of the most prominent firms was that established by John Holmes, an implement maker at Scoles Green, close to the cattle market and his potential customers. Holmes made a variety of agricultural equipment and steam engines, which he exhibited frequently at agricultural shows to attract customers. His exhibits won many awards. When the Royal Agricultural Show was held in Norwich in 1851 the firm displayed 112 items on its stand. By 1862 Holmes had built a new works on Castle Hill facing the cattle market. Known as the Prospect Place Works it employed about 100 men and contained workshops, a large foundry and an imposing glass and iron showroom that still survives. During the late 1880s Holmes and Sons had expanded the range of their goods and advertised themselves as engineers, millwrights, and manufacturers of threshing and dressing machines, stationary engines and drainage turbines. Their success was relatively short-lived – business declined towards the end of the nineteenth century and the firm was declared bankrupt in 1902. Three years later the showroom was taken over by Panks, who would develop their electrical contracting business there.

There were several other engineers and iron founders in Norwich, including engine maker James Watts in Rose Lane and the Sabberton

Opposite:
Holmes'
showroom (later
used by Panks).

Brothers who ran a foundry at the St Martins Palace Iron Works. The city also had many millwrights and several boat builders, such as the Petch family who built wherries by the river at Barrack Street whilst also running the nearby Horse Barracks public house.

Before the coming of the railway to Norwich in 1844, coach travel was the main mode of transport for goods and passengers, and the city had several coach and cart makers. Some survived and become well known for the specialist vehicles they built, including Jolly and Sons in St Stephens, and the Howes family whose business would survive to become part of the motor age.

GAS AND ELECTRICITY

The development of gas lighting and later electricity (for lighting and power), brought the need for engineers able to provide and service the specialist equipment. By 1814 a shop in the market place was lit by gas, produced by burning coal on a stove at the rear of the premises. Within four years Oxley's textile factory on Gentlemans

Walk was lit by gas supplied from its own gasometer. By the late 1830s about four miles of the major roads in the city were lit by gas and plans were in hand to illuminate a further eight miles. Although it provided better lighting than that made by burning tallow or oil, gas was not universally popular – the smell of burning oil or coal gas was unpleasant in confined spaces and there was the ever-present risk of explosion. Electricity was safer and easier to control. In 1880 the Norwich Town Council took the first tentative steps to provide electric street lighting by erecting two lights in the market place, before extending it to some of the principal streets in the city a year later. It was Jeremiah James Colman who recognised the benefits electricity could bring to his business. He employed the Hammond Electric Light and Power Company to provide electric lighting for the roadways at his Carrow works before installing it in the printing department. The power was provided by a dynamo attached to a Riches and Watt 12 horsepower steam engine and each of the four floors was illuminated with 50 small light bulbs.

Opposite:
Holme's Prospect
Place works in
1862.
Left: A Boulton
and Paul
aeroplane being
transported
to Mousehold
in 1922.

> **The techniques of building horse-drawn carriages were utilised in making car bodies.**

The increasing demand for electrically powered machinery attracted innovative engineers, in particular William Harding Scott whose company, later to be known as Laurence, Scott and Electromotors is featured as a case study. He started out supplying Colman's Carrow works with dynamos and electric motors and built up an electrical contracting business. In 1899 this side of the business was sold to Gerard Mann who opened new premises at the corner of Queen Street and Bank Plain, where he went into partnership with Hubert Egerton.

MANN EGERTON

Mann Egerton carried out electrical installations in country houses, factories and public buildings and for the Admiralty and War Office. They also entered the motor trade, using modest premises in Prince of Wales Road where they sold, serviced and hired out cars. The cars they sold were all built to the customers' own specifications. Within a decade the Prince of Wales Road premises had been hugely expanded and the company had become agents for many types of new vehicles, selling second-hand cars and providing garage space for 200.

The increasing availability of motor cars meant work for the city's coachbuilders. The techniques of building horse-drawn carriages were utilised in making car bodies by firms such as Howes, who built up a substantial business building and supplying motor vehicles.

BUSSEYS

Other firms entered the business from scratch as in the case of Charles Bussey who began repairing motor vehicles in partnership with the Payne brothers in Palace Street in 1911, possibly at his father's former grocery shop. In 1922 they acquired the nearby iron foundry and general engineering business run by Sabberton Brothers which had got into financial difficulties. Under the Bussey and Sabberton name, the firm obtained a Ford dealership in 1923, allowing it to sell cars, trucks and tractors. It began acquiring properties in the Palace Street and Quayside area to expand the business. A major new venture was the introduction of a tyre remoulding plant which lasted until 1970.

During the Second World War, despite bombing damage, the Palace Street site maintained and repaired vehicles for the Ministry of Supply and provided remoulded types for military vehicles. Post-war expansion saw new offices built at Palace Street and a new garage opened on Thorpe Road. By 1973 the company had an annual turnover of £2 million, was selling 2,000 cars a year and employed 150 staff. In 1976 a commercial vehicle sales and servicing centre was built on a three-acre site at Whiffler Road at a cost of £100,000. This became the firm's headquarters after the Palace Street site was sold in the 1990s. Busseys remains a major car dealer with branches across Norfolk and currently employs about 200 staff in the county.

PANK

Another Norwich firm who entered the motor trade was that founded by Abraham Pank. Based in Pottergate in the middle of the nineteenth century, he traded as a brass worker, gas fitter and bell hanger. Under the direction of his son, Richard, the business provided gas, electrical and sanitary services, supplied gas and oil engines for agricultural use, and undertook sheet metal work. Following the collapse of Holmes and Sons in 1902, Panks bought their Castle Hill showrooms and workshops, retained some of the staff, and began supplying engines formerly made by Holmes. After the First World War, Panks also acquired the long established firm of Riches and Watt.

By the 1930s the business had a wide spread of interests which included the provision of domestic and commercial heating and an auto-electrical department, established in 1933. Panks were also agents for Crossley oil and gas engines, widely used in agriculture for pumping irrigation water. In a new initiative Panks began supplying wireless sets – an aspect of the business that was to prove very successful. After 1945 Panks carried out a number of large electrical installations including the floodlighting at the Boundary Park football ground in Norwich, call systems at the Norfolk and Norwich Hospital and at the Norwich City

College in Ipswich Road. To meet the demand for home entertainment the firm set up a separate division known as Panks Radio which supplied radios, television sets and records from its three Norwich shops in Davey Place, Orford Place and Prince of Wales Road.

Currently Panks Pumps, based at the old Tannery in Heigham Street, operates across East Anglia with offices at Ipswich and Peterborough. They provide a comprehensive service for sewage, water treatment, food processing and irrigation which includes installation, servicing and repairs. There is a separate auto-electrical division based in Heigham Street.

CHANGE OF DIRECTION

The end of the nineteenth century meant a change of direction for the major Norwich engineering firms. Demand for traditional products such as wire netting declined as former export markets developed their own industries and imposed tariffs on imports. One area of growth was the manufacture of prefabricated buildings. Barnards, and Boulton and Paul had been making them for agricultural and domestic use within Great Britain but now began exporting them, particularly to the countries within the British Empire. By 1900 Boulton and Paul was making glasshouses, orangeries, vineries and palm houses, including a local order for a large conservatory, boiler and piping for the Plantation Garden in Norwich. The second Anglo-Boer war, which broke out in October 1899, generated orders for barracks to accommodate the large numbers of British soldiers sent to South Africa. Many were fabricated in Norwich before being shipped out for erection. The First World War brought massive increases in orders. Barnards supplied thousands of miles of wire netting used in Egypt for road making and to support trench walls, castings for the Admiralty, and cooking stoves for military camps. Boulton and Paul provided military buildings including aircraft hangars, hospitals in England and France, and also marine engines.

In 1915 as part of government efforts to increase the production of military aircraft, both Boulton and Paul and Mann Egerton were asked to make them. Boulton and Paul made parts at Rose Lane which were assembled by coachbuilders employed by Howes and Sons. The semi-finished aircraft were then transported to an airstrip laid out on the old Cavalry training ground on Mousehold Heath for final assembly and test flights. In an effort to streamline the production process a new factory was put up at a three-acre site on Riverside in 1916. It took only three months to build. In all, Boulton and Paul made over 2,500 aircraft in Norwich during the war including Sopwith Camels, Snipes and FE2s. The firm's other major contribution to the war effort was the part it played in making fuses for shells. It was one of the partners in a company known as Norwich Components which made over two million fuses – for a period they had to be assembled at the St Giles skating rink after the original factory was destroyed by fire. Mann Egerton also put up a new factory. In 1916, with the assistance of a large loan from the War Office, a 60-acre site was purchased on Cromer Road just north of Norwich where a large hangar was quickly built and an airfield laid out. The company also maintained thousands of tractors to assist the war effort.

The post-war period brought major changes – especially for those firms with large workforces who had been engaged in war work; Mann Egerton alone had 1,200 people making aircraft. They utilised their war-time experience of maintaining agricultural equipment and began selling and servicing tractors and other agricultural equipment. The firm also utilized the woodworking skills their staff had developed when building aircraft to begin making furniture. This would become an important part of the business and Mann Egerton became a major supplier of school furniture. The firm also began making bodies for motor coaches and commercial vehicles.

Below: An aerial view of Boulton and Paul's Riverside works in 1939.

THE RIVERSIDE WORKS

At the end of the First World War, Boulton and Paul decided to concentrate all manufacturing at the Riverside site. The Rose Lane factory was sold to the Co-operative Wholesale Society for use as a shoe factory. The firm overcame the post-war slump by concentrating on three main areas – woodworking, making structural steelwork for the construction industry at home and abroad, and wire netting, although wire netting was not as profitable as it had been before the war.

In a brave venture the company also decided to make their own aircraft, designed by John Dudley North who was convinced that he could produce all-metal aircraft for both military and civilian use. His first all-metal plane, the P10, was displayed at the Salon de l'Aeronautique at Paris in 1919 and caused a stir. North went on to design a number of successful military aircraft including the Sidestrand and Overstrand bombers for the Royal Air Force. The structure for the ill-fated airship the R101, which crashed on its maiden flight outside the UK killing most of the people on board, was also made at Riverside.

The depression of the early 1930s hit Boulton and Paul hard as its key markets – agriculture, the building trade and public works – cut back on orders and the company began to lose money. In 1932 it was reorganised into four divisions – structural steel, aircraft, woodworking and wire weaving – and a new management structure put in place. Two years later it was decided to dispose of the aircraft-making division and a new company, Boulton Paul Aircraft, was established with a share capital of £300,000. The new company was set up as part of government proposals to increase the capacity of the aircraft manufacturing industry and was located in Wolverhampton, away from the east coast and the threat of aerial attack.

Opposite:
Boulton and
Paul's offices
on Rose Lane.

As the country emerged from recession, Boulton and Paul returned to profitability. It had developed an expertise in erecting steel structures, initially farm buildings but later large commercial premises such as airport terminals, cinemas and theatres. The firm also worked on government projects including the construction of a wind tunnel at the Royal Aircraft Establishment at Farnborough, and built armaments factories as part of preparations for war.

WAR EFFORT

Once war was declared in September 1939, the city's engineering factories were rapidly involved in the war effort. Boulton and Paul made wooden buildings for army camps, parts for gliders, radio masts and 40-ton trailers for tank transporters. Mann Egerton turned out over 4,000 military vehicles and repaired thousands more. They continued to make furniture, much of which replaced that lost in air raids. Barnards employed over 1,200 people at its Mousehold factory making artillery shells, aircraft parts and wire netting for airfield runways. Both Barnards, and Boulton and Paul suffered from air raids in which employees were killed and factory buildings damaged.

The end of the war brought a period of sustained prosperity. In Norwich, engineering remained an important industry and a major employer for at least 20 years before takeovers and closures led to its virtual disappearance.

Barnards was the first to lose its independence. By 1947 its pre-war workforce had halved and to supplement wire weaving began making industrial trailers and steel racking for the shoe industry. The company also began making commercial baking ovens, including one for a Scottish customer which was over 90 feet long and capable of turning out 2,400 large loaves an hour. Within two years the workforce was up to 600, divided between the Coslany Street foundry and wire works, and the Mousehold factory.

The foundry was sold in 1953 and production of wire netting moved to Mousehold. New types of netting were developed including PVC covered netting for the making of gabions and breakwaters to prevent coastal erosion, galvanised wire netting for the offshore oil industry and ornamental garden fencing known as Norlink.

In 1955 Barnards was bought by Sheffield-based Tinsley Wire Industries. The new owners continued production at Mousehold, and nine years later added Boulton and Paul's wire weaving division to their empire at a cost of £370,000, merging it with Barnards. In 1976 the firm celebrated their 150th anniversary. It would not see its 200th as in March 1990 Tinsley announced that due to falling sales, production of wire netting would be moved to Sheffield and the Norwich factory would close, although the 100 men to lose their jobs would be offered work in Sheffield. Barnard's Mousehold factory finally closed in December 1990 and the Salhouse Road site is now occupied by a retail park and a DIY store.

BOULTON AND PAUL – TAKEOVER AND CLOSURE

After 1945 Boulton and Paul concentrated on making doors and windows for the building industry, and steel fabrication for buildings, increasing its productive capacity by taking over the Melton Mowbray-based Midland Woodworking Company. In 1948 a controlling interest in the firm was purchased by Anglo Transvaal Industries, a South African mining and building materials company, but its headquarters remained in Norwich and it continued to be listed on the London Stock Exchange. The 1950s saw further expansion including a brief excursion into the pre-cast concrete business and takeovers of scaffolding companies and other door manufacturers. In 1962 a new factory was built at Lowestoft at a cost of almost £1 million where components would be machined for assembly at the Norwich and Melton Mowbray factories.

In September 1968 the *Eastern Daily Press* reported that British Electric Traction, a massive conglomerate later known as BET, had acquired 51% of the voting shares in Boulton and Paul. The new owners promised that the jobs of the company's 3,000 workers were secure but the 1970s saw redundancies, the end of aluminium window making at Riverside, and a cut back in the manufacture of joinery. In 1981 alone over 300 jobs were lost due to a lack of demand for structural steelwork. Finally, five years later, all steel work production finished and in November 1986 the Riverside joinery works closed with the loss of the remaining 240 jobs.

By February 1990 BET had reconsidered its priorities, decided it no longer wanted to make joinery and offered Boulton and Paul for sale along with Norwich double glazing manufacturer Anglian Windows, which it had bought from its founder George Williams only six years earlier. There was little interest and the business was retained, only to be sold three years later to the existing management team in a £14.5 million buyout. BET were glad to be rid of Boulton and Paul; it had lost £9.5 million in the year to March 1992 and was on course for an even bigger loss in the year it was sold.

As BET had done, the new owners announced there would be no redundancies, either at the Norwich head office which still employed 144 people, or at the Lowestoft factory which employed more than 350 workers making windows and doors. In 1993 the head office moved from Riverside to the Pinetrees Business Park at Sprowston. After extensive decontamination work, the Riverside site was cleared for work to begin on a major shopping, leisure and housing development. The new owners were unable to stem the losses and the company was sold again in March 1997 to the Rugby Group who, despite cutting over 750 jobs, were unable to return the company to profitability. They sold it on in 1999 to Jeld Wen, a large American manufacturer of doors and windows and the name Boulton and Paul was dropped.

MANN EGERTON INCHED OUT

Mann Egerton lost its independence in 1973 when an offer of £17.5 million for the company from Inchcape was accepted by the directors. At the time the business employed over 5,000 people nationally and was a major distributor of British Leyland and Rolls Royce cars. It had a large repair and car hire business, made furniture and was a major electrical contractor. During the previous five years it had expanded substantially. It was an attractive target for Inchcape who wished to expand its UK car sales business and so like Boulton and Paul, the Mann Egerton name disappeared.

AUTOWRAPPERS

Amid the gloom over the decline of the city's traditional engineering businesses there was some cause for optimism. Autowrappers was very much a post-war success story – but one with a sad ending. The company developed a range of innovative food-wrapping machines which were exported across the world. The business was started by Charles Maddison and his partner H. E. Martin who in 1946 bought the semi-derelict premises of the former Norwich Crape Company in Edward Street for

£12,500. There, with four staff, they began developing wrapping machines. Maddison had been an engineer with Mackintoshs so was familiar with the requirements of the confectionary industry. He had tried making wrapping machines during the 1930s in a hired garage in Leeds, but without success.

As the orders began to come in, the firm found temporary additional space at a former aircraft hangar at Mousehold. By 1954 the Edward Street site had been extended by the building of a 12,300 square foot machine-making shop, bringing all the operations together on one site. All the parts required were made by the firm's own engineers, apart from castings which were made elsewhere in Norwich. The 120-strong workforce was turning out up to 12 machines each month, ranging in value from £500 to £2,500 each. From the earliest days much of the output had been exported – the first machine had been supplied to a confectionary factory in Madras – and they were soon being sold to over 20 countries. Autowrappers would turn out whatever the customer required – from sandwich sealing machines for caterers to a machine that could wrap magazines in polythene ready for posting.

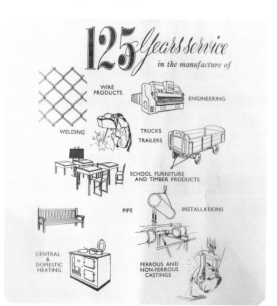

Left: Barnard's products as advertised in 1953.

Below: A chocolate-wrapping system made by Autowrappers in 1990.

In 1958 Maddison decided to sell Autowrappers, He was 58 and had devoted much of his life to making Autowrappers a success. It was bought by Tobenoil, a public company with other packaging interests. In a remarkable gesture Maddison gave £15,000 to his staff in cash and shares as a 'thank you' – one employee was reported to have received £1,000. That year the company announced it had filled orders from over 40 countries, including the USSR and China.

The concentration on exports continued under the new owners and by the early 1960s, 70% of its production was going abroad, much to Europe but also to the United States, Russia and Japan. In 1963 the factory floor area was increased by 25% and the firm began looking for further expansion. To combat the scarcity of skilled engineers, Autowrappers considered establishing its own training school – both for training school leavers and retraining older people transferring from other industries. The following year saw the company recruiting 20 engineers from outside Norwich and asking the City Council to provide housing for them.

Lack of space at Edward Street was restricting expansion so in 1965 a completely new factory was built on the outskirts of the city at Drayton Road at a cost of £200,000. Opened in March 1966 it had 40,000 square feet of production space with an adjacent four-acre site set aside for future expansion. The new factory employed 200 – mainly machinists, fitters, toolmakers and sheet metal workers, along with design and sales staff. The company now made five basic machines for a range of uses including roll wrapping of confectionary, packaging and cartoning of chocolate and pharmaceuticals, plus labelling machines and sleeving equipment for the canning industry. One rather exotic product was a candle maker – it could make 480 candles in 20 minutes; Autowrappers was the only firm in the UK that made them.

The company's continued success led to an additional 17,000 square feet of production space being added in 1975 to meet the overseas orders that continued to flow in. Autowrappers had also established an apprenticeship scheme in partnership with Norwich City College. The United States was a particularly profitable market with orders for confectionary wrapping machines worth over £300,000 being received during the early 1970s. In 1977 an order worth £210,000 from Australia was received. By then Autowrappers' parent company, Tobenoil, had been taken over by GEI International, a specialist engineering group based in Bedfordshire. Autowrappers continued to flourish throughout the 1980s – culminating in a massive order worth £2.5 million from Rowntrees in 1989 for machines to wrap their Fruit Pastilles. This was followed in 1990 by an even larger order from the United States for chocolate-wrapping machines.

Faced with increasing competition, Autowrappers began developing fully automated wrapping systems in place of the individual machines they had traditionally made. Some were able to wrap up to 800 chocolate bars an hour and handle a variety of sizes. Over £300,000 was spent in October 1990 to provide a computer-aided design system to develop new machinery in an attempt to remain competitive. However, difficult market conditions meant that the company asked for 42 voluntary redundancies out of its 215-strong workforce. Three years later Autowrappers was merged with Europak, another GEI company based at Beccles. Both factories remained open, and by the following year work had picked up with orders worth £9 million received and new engineers being recruited.

Sadly, this proved a false dawn and by 1999 the company's position was precarious. In May GEI announced that, following the discovery of a shortfall of some £3 million in Autowrappers accounts, several senior managers had left the company, production would be moving from Norwich, and the Drayton Road factory was to be sold. After the closure the factory stood empty for some years before the site was used for car sales.

BALDING ENGINEERING

In many ways the story of Balding Engineering mirrors that of Autowrappers – modest beginnings, an innovative product, success built on the vision of one man, continuous development to meet changing needs, an export success story, but a sad end. A profile of Victor Balding, founder of the firm, published in 1958 at the time Balding Engineering was about to move to a new factory on Sweet Briar Road, recalled how the company had grown dramatically since its formation in 1951 to a business that was selling its machine tools across the world.

Victor was a farmer's son from Terrington St John with little formal education who had trained as a fitter at Laurence, Scott and Electromotors in Norwich, before becoming the manager of a small engineering works at March in Cambridgeshire. He had always wanted to be in business for himself and in 1951 took the plunge, exchanging the security of his March job to sink his £7,000 savings into a new venture in Norwich. The Balding Engineering Company began life making machine tools in a workshop on Duke Street that had once been the power station which supplied electricity to the Norwich tram network. Within four years he was

Above: An interior view of the Balding Engineering factory in 1960. Below: A view of the workshop.

employing 30 men and had outgrown the site. Balding bought a site at Bessemer Road where a 4,000 square foot factory for making the firm's swivelling turret milling machine was built. Within three years it had tripled in size.

A major breakthrough came in 1960, when, after exhibiting at the London Machine Tool Exhibition, orders worth £70,000 were received, helping the firm's turnover to reach £250,000. Balding machines all bore the distinctive Beaver trademark devised by Balding's wife. The company could not keep up with demand, due to the lack of suitable skilled labour available and production space. This was partially addressed when a former barrel factory in Great Yarmouth was taken over to make components.

In 1961 the company moved its main factory again, to a site on Sweet Briar Road. Victor Balding not only designed the building but helped construct it. Originally covering 25,000 square feet, within a few years it had grown threefold. About 600 turret milling machines, designed by Balding and a colleague, were made annually with many going to European Union countries, where West Germany was the biggest market. By January 1964, 80% of the company's output was being exported, the 200-strong workforce was working two shifts to meet demand and orders from 35 countries were in hand. Within months the workforce had increased by 50 and three new bays were added to the production area. That December the company estimated that about 3,000 Beaver milling machines were in use across the world, mainly in the United States, Canada, Australia and West Germany. A new office block was built the following year to accommodate the office and design staff.

To meet demand for milling machines, a subsidiary factory was established on a former airfield at Little Snoring near Fakenham in 1965. Production of milling machines reached 1,000 a year by August of 1967 and the firm was optimistic it would soon be making 1,700. Three types of milling machine were made with either standard, numerical or electronic controls. Balding Engineering proudly claimed that their machines were all British, with all the components, apart from castings and electrics which were made elsewhere in the UK, manufactured by the company. A new development was the automatic Beavermatic whose production cycle was controlled by punched tape. It was claimed to be the first completely automatic machining centre.

The firm's success, especially in the export trade, was due in no small part to the drive and commitment of Victor Balding who travelled thousands of miles selling machines and attending trade fairs in Europe, America and South Africa. During 1966 he estimated he had travelled 100,000 miles. His efforts bore fruit, particularly in the United States where by 1967 Baldings were supplying almost half of all the milling machines imported into the country. In recognition, the company was awarded the Queen's Award to Industry for export achievement that year.

THE BUSY BEAVER

The 20 years that followed were a golden age for Balding Engineering. By 1968 it was employing 350, a tenfold increase on the number a decade before and had 112,000 square feet of production space. That August an order from Balding's Los Angeles distributor for 232 machines worth £150,000 was received. In 1970 the company became Beaver Engineering in recognition of the success of its Beaver trademark by which it was commonly known. Despite a slight downturn in 1972, which forced the closure of the Little Snoring factory, the company was going from strength to strength. In its search for skilled labour it was forced to recruit outside Norwich.

Beaver was established as the only British company in its particular field of precision mechanical engineering and some of the country's largest engineering companies, including Marconi, Rolls-Royce, GEC and Hawker Siddley, used Beaver milling machines. By now Tony Balding had joined his father as joint managing directors of Beaver. Its products ranged from the basic manual turret milling machine costing about £3,000 to programmable fully automatic machines, such as the NC15 bed-type vertical machine centre, which once set up could conduct complicated sequences of drilling, turning and milling required to make machine parts in a fraction of the time it would have taken an operator. Much of the development work on the new range had been carried out by the company's own design department which had been established in 1974.

There was further expansion in June 1984 when Beaver leased 10,000 square feet of factory space in Peterborough to make parts for assembly at Norwich. The company announced it would be recruiting up to 15 skilled machine tool operators, targeting those recently made redundant following the closure of Newall's Peterborough factory. Additional space for sub-assembly work was also rented in Halesworth two years later. In April 1988 Beaver announced the company would be moving from Sweet Briar Road to a new purpose-built factory not far away at Bowthorpe. The new building provided the space to build the larger and heavier machines that were being designed. It was also likely to lead to the employment of a further 100 staff in addition to the existing 215. The factory was ready in August 1990. It had 104,000 square feet on a seven and a half acre site at Barnard Road and cost £4 million. Its construction had not been straightforward. When the developer got into difficulties Beaver had been forced to take over construction of the factory.

However, the cost of building the new factory and the challenging economic conditions of the early 1990s had strained the company's finances. Turnover reached £11 million in 1987 generating an operating profit of just over £1 million, but the following years saw substantial losses as the recession started to bite and sales in the UK dropped off. Despite increasing export sales, now taking 60% of the company's output, and its new CNC machining centres which were attracting much interest, Beaver Engineering was in serious trouble. The end came suddenly on 14th July 1992 when the company was put into receivership by its bank NatWest after being unable to repay its overdraft. It was a disaster for Beaver and the Balding family who had spent over 40 years building up the business. It was a disaster for Norwich who lost the UK's leading machine tool makers and it was a disaster for the workforce, as 82 of the firm's employees were made redundant immediately whilst the remaining 50 went in October when the company was sold to a Swiss machine tool maker. The Barnard Road factory was later sold by the receivers.

Right: Construction of the new Beaver Engineering factory at Bowthorpe underway in 1990.

DIAMOND H

One of the more heartening post-war developments was the arrival in Norwich in 1964 of Diamond H Controls who moved from Chiswick to make use of the large pool of semi-skilled labour available in the city. The US-owned firm made electrical switch gear for cookers and other domestic appliances and had factories in the US, Canada, Australia and South Africa.

Whilst a new 75,000 square foot factory was being built on Vulcan Road North, Diamond H used the former Hurrell's shoe factory in Magdalen Street. The new factory opened in November 1964 and soon employed 300. Over the next few years new products were introduced and staff numbers increased so that by 1967 the factory employed 550. A further 50 key staff had moved from Chiswick and there were ambitious plans for expansion. The company supplied manufacturers such as Belling, Creda and Tricity. Most of its output was sold within the UK and some exported to New Zealand. The company also produced membrane switches for computers, microwaves and laboratory equipment.

In 1969 a further 35,000 square feet of production space was added and by 1976 the Vulcan Road factory was employing over 800. Demand for the company's switches was such that branch factories had been set up at Mildenhall and Brandon. This success was short-lived. In September 1979 the branch factories were closed and 200 laid off at Norwich. Diamond H was sold in 1990 to the Yale and Valor Group for some £6.5 million. Yale and Valor already owned Norwich-based Heatrae and claimed that they would be investing in Diamond H, but within a year it had been sold on to Williams Holdings. At that point Diamond H had been hit hard by the recession and its workforce was down to 400. Within three years it had been sold again, this time in a management buyout to Cortworth. Diamond H no longer makes switches in Norwich but has a head office in Coventry and manufactures controls for domestic appliances at Shenzhen in China.

TODAY

In 2013 Norwich still has an engineering industry, albeit on a considerably smaller scale than 50 years ago. ATB Laurence Scott is a world leader in the manufacture of electric motors for the oil, gas and energy industries, Panks has adapted to a world very different to that of Abraham Pank when he founded the firm in the 1850s, whilst Ben Burgess continues in the tradition of the Norwich iron founders and implement makers in supplying equipment to the county's famers.

Reminders of the city's engineering industry can still be seen. Holmes and Sons' original showrooms still stand on Market Avenue, the Boulton and Paul offices on Rose Lane now provide housing, whilst the name of Bishop, Barnard and Bishop is still proudly displayed on the St Crispin's Bridge.

Left: The production line at Diamond H in 1988.

LAURENCE, SCOTT & ELECTROMOTORS

William Harding Scott was an extraordinary man. He built a business in Norwich that was quite unlike anything that had gone before it, one that became pre-eminent in its field and one that continues to be successful today as ATB Laurence Scott. His genius lay in recognising the potential of electricity as a source of motive power in industry. Scott was an inventor but also a perfectionist whose determination to solve the problems he encountered was legendary.

The scope of his activities was impressive and his ability to find practical solutions to technical problems gave Laurence Scott an international reputation. After his initial work on dynamos, Scott turned his hand to the generation and supply of electricity, building electric motors, making control gear and switchgear, steering gear, winches for marine

Above: William Harding Scott in his office.

use, and cutting and tunnelling equipment. Just before his death in 1938, the company had developed some of the earliest traffic lights in the UK which were installed in Norwich.

At his death Scott had built a company which had a worldwide reputation for its electric motors, winches and control gear. Furthermore he had established it in an area with no tradition of heavy industry, far from the factories and shipyards it supplied.

SCOTT ARRIVES IN NORWICH

It appears Scott first came to Norwich in 1883 when his employer, the Hammond Electric Light and Power Company, was installing electric lighting to illuminate the roadways and printing works at Colman's Carrow works. Supervised by Edward Paris, Hammond's electrician, it used a 12 horsepower Riches and Watt steam engine to drive a dynamo which in turn provided enough power to light 50 small lamps strung on wires. It was claimed that each lamp would last for about 1,000 hours before the carbon coil had to be replaced.

The firm's proprietor, Robert Hammond, took the opportunity to extol the benefits of electric lighting by giving a lecture at the Agricultural Hall in April 1883. The hall was lit by the new lighting and the press reported that it produced 'a pure and remarkably steady blaze of light illuminating the stage with a radiancy that made no addition at lighting in the area of the room necessary'.

Once the work at Carrow was completed Paris and Scott remained in Norwich, setting themselves up in business as Paris & Scott at a workshop in King Street that they rented from Colman. Edward Paris was a German who lived in Norwich for at least eight years and later worked for the Brush Electrical Company. The workshop near Dragon Hall was later known as the Gothic Works due to its castle-like appearance. Colman also helped Scott personally by renting him a cottage on Bracondale.

By the 1880s the possibilities of electricity were evident – initially as a source of lighting to replace the smelly and dangerous gas lighting, but also as a source of power in workshops and factories. Paris and Scott hoped to take advantage of the opportunities this provided but lacked capital. This arrived in the shape of Reginald Laurence, the wealthy son of a stock broker who was looking for somewhere to invest. He put £6,000 into the business, becoming the dominant partner, the firm being renamed Laurence, Paris and Scott. Jeremiah Colman also took an interest, buying 3,000 one pound shares leaving Paris and Scott with 1,000 each. Although Laurence had trained as an engineer with Cockerill's in Liège, his contribution to the business was that of providing stability and discipline and perhaps reining in Scott's determined pursuit of perfection. At the time the King Street premises held a workshop with four lathes and other equipment and a small drawing office where the firm's two draughtsman worked. Edward Paris resigned in 1889 and moved back to London. The firm was renamed Laurence and Scott.

THE BENEFITS OF ELECTRICITY

The new business was soon offered an opportunity to demonstrate its expertise. In 1889 they installed electric lighting powered by a small generating station in the lending and reading rooms of the Free Library in St Andrews to demonstrate its effectiveness. It caused a sensation but more importantly brought in orders for electric lighting. Paris and Scott built a central generating station which supplied electricity via overhead cables. Initially the supply was unmetered with customers being charged a flat rate each quarter.

Lacking the capital required to invest in a large-scale electrification project, Laurence Scott was unable to meet an increasing local demand for electric lighting and in 1891 the Norwich Electricity Company was formed to supply the city. Scott designed the generating station and the distribution system which consisted of bare copper mains supported by earthenware insulators within iron pipes. By 1896 seven miles of new mains had been laid throughout the city and the efficiency and reliability of Scott's system enabled the new business to make money.

Freed from the distractions of running an electrical distribution business, Laurence Scott concentrated on making and selling electric motors and dynamos built to the customer's specifications, and on general electrical contracting. Orders from home and abroad began to flow in as the firm developed a reputation for the quality of its workmanship and its ability to come up with innovative solutions. By 1889 the Gothic Works employed some 25 men and Scott was turning his attention to making electric motors for ships, an important component of the firm's output in the years ahead.

Opposite:
The Gothic
Works in 1908.

A NEW GOTHIC WORKS

The 1890s was a decade of change for Laurence Scott. The Gothic Works was not large enough to cope with the increasing workload and it was clear the company required further capital to maintain its expansion. In 1896 a new company was formed with a share capital of £50,000 which included 50 founders' shares of one pound each, which gave the holders enhanced profit sharing rights compared with the other shareholders. The directors of the new company were Scott, Laurence, Cecil Wilson and Charles Burlingham. Wilson, an accountant, was Laurence's brother-in-law who, on Laurence's death in 1923, would take his place as Chairman. Burlingham was Jeremiah Colman's accountant, maintaining the close link with the Colmans.

That same year, work began on a new factory, laid out on a site bought from Colman's on the north bank of the river opposite Carrow works, and named the Gothic Works to perpetuate the links with the original factory. It covered an area of some 7,500 square feet with work bays arranged around a large yard to facilitate ease

of manufacture and was supplied by electricity generated on site. The new works employed about 100 men. Time keeping was strictly enforced although if a man worked a full 52-hour week without time off he was paid for 54. When the works opened in 1898 the lease on the King Street works was relinquished.

In 1899 it was decided to dispense with the electrical contracting side which had grown substantially. The stock and goodwill was bought by Gerald Mann for £6,000 and Laurence Scott gave an undertaking not to engage in electrical contracting in Norfolk for five years.

MAKING MOTORS

Laurence Scott now concentrated on making electric motors and control gear for civilian and military use. New applications were developed for the use of electric power which required specialist combinations of motors and control gear, such as ammunition hoists for warships. As the company gained expertise in making military equipment, orders came in from Vickers, Maxims and the Admiralty.

However, the largest order received during 1899 was for a power station at Lincoln where Laurence Scott supplied engines, dynamos, condensers and other equipment. The next few years saw further orders for power stations at Epsom, King's Lynn and Lowestoft. That year the company filled 500 orders and made a profit of £7,000, thanks to an increase in demand for its electric motors. However, in the face of increased competition the firm found it difficult to maintain quality whilst remaining competitive on price.

In 1902 Laurence Scott entered into an agreement with Electromotors – a Manchester-based maker of small electric motors. Scotts agreed not to bid for orders for the motors Electromotors specialised in and in return Electromotors agreed not to bid for orders for larger motors. The two companies would also sell motors to one another at favourable prices. Scotts subsequently discovered they were able to manufacture the smaller motors for less than Electromotors could supply them so the agreement lapsed.

By 1905 the economic climate had deteriorated. Much of the workforce was working reduced hours and there had been redundancies. Despite this the directors continued to invest in the business, building a new test shop on land bought from Colman's. As tension increased between Great Britain and Germany, orders from the Admiralty boosted business and by 1907 the order book was three times what it had been two years earlier. The workforce grew accordingly to meet the demand. In 1907, 430 were employed at the Gothic Works. Within three years it was up to 550.

By then about 1,000 machines a year were being made and Laurence Scott was gaining a national reputation, being described as 'a firm which makes very high class electric motors'. Output remained at this level for several years but the motors became larger and more complex.

In 1913 the company celebrated its 25th anniversary with a garden party held at Felthorpe Hall, the home of Reginald Laurence. Gifts of travelling clocks or timepieces were made to members of staff, with the three longest serving being given gold watches.

WORK FOR THE ADMIRALTY

The outbreak of war in August 1914 brought a change of emphasis for Laurence Scott. Orders for civilian work dried up and work for the Admiralty took precedence as the company made motors, ammunition hoists, mechanisms for turning warship turrets and other marine equipment. There was also a major change in the make-up of the workforce. By October 1914 a quarter of the men had enlisted and for the first time women were employed at the Gothic Works.

In common with the other Norwich engineering factories, Laurence Scott was asked to produce munitions. Construction of two sheds began in late 1915 and new tools were devised to enable semi-skilled workers to make artillery shells. By 1916 around 250 three-inch and five-inch shells were being made each day for the war effort. At the end of the war it was estimated that Laurence Scott had made about £1 million worth of shells 'from home made tools in two corrugated tin sheds'.

The peace brought a brief boom and the company invested in the anticipation of the good times continuing – the Gothic Works was expanded, and a large private house and its grounds on Thorpe Road became the control gear works. Later a foundry was added. Agencies were established to sell Laurence Scott motors in the UK and links established with the Netherlands to sell motors to shipbuilders there.

Opposite,
top to bottom:
The pattern shop

and foundry at
Laurence Scott
in the 1920s.

The boom proved to be short-lived and was followed by a severe slump. Orders dropped off, prices had to be reduced and work was taken on at uneconomic prices to keep the business going. In June 1922 a salary cut of 10% was imposed to reduce the wage bill but, despite this, the business was running at only a quarter of its pre-war peak and carrying a substantial overdraft. In July 1923 the company's chairman, Reginald Laurence, died at a London nursing home at the age of 66. He was a great loss. Alongside his role at Laurence Scott, he had thrown himself wholeheartedly into the life of his adopted county and in particular the Norfolk and Norwich Hospital where he was a member of the Board of Management and a generous benefactor. During the First World War he and his wife Cisley turned over their home at Felthorpe Hall to the Red Cross for use as a hospital. By the time it was returned to their full use in January 1919 its 23 beds had accommodated many military casualties. His position on the board of directors was taken by his nephew, Claud Laurence, a stockbroker.

As the economy began to improve, orders for marine equipment helped Laurence Scott recover and by 1924 the firm was breaking even. The Scott winch, developed in 1922, was a bestseller with 30 being sold in the first year. By 1925 over 100 were sold, many to Belfast shipbuilders Harland and Wolff but others to Japan, the Netherlands and France. It was reliable, long-lasting and required minimal maintenance. It was also relatively silent, a useful attribute when fitted to the passenger cargo liners then being built. By 1932 about 200 were being sold annually. Much business was done with Belfast shipbuilders Harland and Wolf – in 1920 they took over 60% of Laurence Scott's output. However, not everything was going well. The electrical engineering side was not so quick to recover and struggled throughout the 1920s. In 1928 Laurence Scott took over Manchester-based Electromotors, paying for it with £50,000 worth of Laurence Scott shares and renaming the business

Laurence, Scott and Electromotors (LSE). Electromotors had been making losses for some years. Its factory was antiquated, but its range of small electric motors was a useful addition to the LSE catalogue and it had experience of making induction motors. This proved useful as LSE moved from making motors powered by direct current (DC) to those powered by alternating current (AC). AC motors and generators were simpler, more reliable and less costly to manufacture. They were also safer as they did not rely on coils making intermittent contact with the brushes as DC motors did, which generated heat and produced the possibility of sparking, a major problem if the working environment contained flammable vapours.

> During the war, the company produced submarine motors, sound locators and searchlights for air defences, and plotted tables and ammunition hoists for the Royal Navy.

SUPPLYING THE QUEEN MARY

Just as the company was emerging from the post-war slump, the worldwide economic depression of the early 1930s hit it hard. A reduction in shipbuilding orders and in particular the suspension of work on the Queen Mary and Queen Elizabeth in December 1931, which would have used Laurence Scott motors, winches and control gear, was a huge setback and yet again salary cuts were imposed. Still driven by the ever inventive William Scott, the company investigated new products. One was the country's first vehicle-controlled traffic lights, activated by cars passing over rubber pads set in the road. Designed by Scott, the first set were installed in the 1930s at the junction of Unthank Road and Colman Road in Norwich and later used throughout the UK. LSE also developed plotting tables for the Admiralty, used for plotting the positions of enemy ships and aircraft, and motors for diesel electric railway locomotives.

By 1935 a trading loss of £35,000 suffered during the previous year had been turned into a profit of £15,000, although the company was carrying a £73,000 bank loan. The next few years saw a steady improvement as turnover increased, greatly helped by government orders as the country rearmed. For the financial year 1936, for the first time since 1929, a dividend was paid to the shareholders and capital was invested in extending the Norwich and Manchester factories. The following year saw a 50% increase in production. The number of employees rose to 3,000 and the dividend payable to the shareholders was doubled. A source of great pride and something the company made much of in its advertising was the use of LSE equipment on the Queen Mary and Queen Elizabeth when work re-started in 1934.

In September 1938 the death of William Scott at his home on Yarmouth Road, aged 76, brought an era to a close. He had been in poor health for about a year, and a few weeks before had suffered the death of his youngest son Thomas. As his obituary in the *Eastern Daily Press* commented, William had been 'one of the pioneers of the electrical industry, starting before there was any electrical industry as we understand it now and building up in his lifetime a great firm…sending its products to all parts of the world'.

By the time war arrived in 1939 profits had risen to £123,000. The firm was effectively on a war footing before 1939, producing submarine motors, sound locators and searchlights for air defences, and plotting tables and ammunition hoists for the Royal Navy. Much of the naval equipment had to function in a harsh environment so had to be much more robust that the motors made for civilian use. Women were recruited as men joined the armed services.

THIRTY YEARS OF SUCCESS

After 1945 there was no post-war slump for LSE but the beginning of a period of sustained success which lasted for 30 years. As of the 31st December 1945 LSE had total net assets of over £750,000. In 1946 the company issued 250,000 one pound shares to buy new plant and materials and to finance the changeover from war production to peacetime manufacturing. The well-established marine side continued to flourish with orders being received from across the world, whilst at home LSE winches were installed on most British-built trawlers. In a return to its origins, the company began supplying motors to power stations. Within the UK alone over 30 coal, oil and nuclear power stations were supplied, including Windscale and Sizewell B. There was diversification into new fields, such as the factory at Kingsbury, near Wolverhampton, which designed, manufactured and installed printing equipment. In 1959 a factory was built at Blantyre in Scotland to make small electric motors for ventilation fans.

Additional production space was found in Norwich. A new site was leased at Salhouse Road for machining, casemaking and pattern making. A new heavy machinery bay was built at the Gothic Works to provide space for large motors in 1959, and in the 1960s the Thorpe Road works was extended. In 1961, to secure the skilled engineers it needed, the company established an apprentice training school, retaining most of those who finished their apprenticeships. By 1973, of around 500 school leavers in the Norwich area, 67 joined LSE as apprentices.

LSE celebrated its 75th anniversary in 1958, no mean feat as it was one of the few original firms in the electrical engineering industry still surviving in the UK. Not only surviving but prospering. In their annual report for 1959 the directors could report on orders of 'a long term nature', for ships' winches, traction generators and motors for British Railways.

By 1977 LSE had a turnover of £28.61 million, up from £25.25 million the previous year, with pre-tax profits of £2.75 million which the chairman Paul Tapscott described as 'The best year's trading in our history'. The company's factories were working at almost full capacity and a £3 million expansion programme was on schedule.

MINING SUPPLIES TAKE OVER

That was as good as it got. A downturn in orders for large electric motors brought reduced profits for 1978. By the end of the following year turnover was down to just under £16 million and the company was facing losses of £1.4 million in the first six months of the year. On the morning of the 19th May 1980 the directors of LSE discovered they were likely to be taken over. A firm of stockbrokers, acting on behalf of Doncaster-based Mining Supplies, had bought 16.4% of the company's shares. Arthur Snipe, the Chairman of Mining Supplies, announced he intended to buy a substantial stake in LSE, with whom his company did a lot of business, to prevent a takeover by anybody else. Mining Supplies had been started by Snipe in 1960 to manufacture mining equipment designed by him and made at their three factories near Doncaster.

Within four months the takeover was completed and the new owners announced a major restructuring to bring the company back into profit. In May 1981 the Manchester factory was closed with the loss of 650 jobs and 90 employees dismissed at Norwich with only two hours' notice. A few months later it was announced that in future the company would concentrate on the profitable areas such as defence equipment and that other departments were at risk.

In August what the new owners described as 'a stringent rationalisation plan' was announced, which would involve large-scale redundancies, the introduction of new machine tools and computer-aided management systems. The apprentice training scheme which was costing the company £600,000 a year was to be reviewed.

The next few years were difficult, both for the company, as its new management fought to return it to profitability, and for the workforce, which was steadily depleted. In 1983 questions were raised about the future of the Thorpe Road works after much of the work was moved to the Gothic Works and more redundancies were announced. It was closed two years later and demolished, to be replaced by the Thorpe Park housing development. By then the workforce was down to about 1,300 – half of what it had been a few years earlier. It was evident that Mining Supplies was losing interest in LSE and in June 1986 it was sold to FKI Electrical in a deal reportedly worth £6.2 million. Mining Supplies had decided that LSE was no longer an essential part of its business and its disposal would permit them to reduce their debts. Mining Supplies retained the Salhouse Road plant.

FKI Electrical was a group of companies which had expanded rapidly by taking over other businesses and had bought the East Dereham clock makers, Metamec, the year before. Yet again, a change of ownership brought more job losses. Within a few weeks notices were put up at the Gothic Works giving staff a few days to apply for voluntary redundancy. Over 300 jobs went, reducing the workforce to about 700. However, the next few years saw substantial investment. In April 1994 FKI announced that the company had spent over £4 million on new equipment at the Gothic Works and, despite a shortage of orders from the defence, power generation and petro-chemical industries, the business was strong and profitable. Indeed, LSE had been expanding, paying £1.8 million to buy Bedford Pumps.

Opposite:
Making electrical
motors in 1962.

So it came as a shock, when in January 2004 LSE announced that due to a shortfall in orders the manufacture of high voltage electric motors would be moved from Norwich and the Gothic Works closed and sold with the loss of 250 jobs. It became apparent that after three years of declining profits FKI was in a desperate financial position with debts of over £500 million. In an attempt to retrieve the situation it was selling four of the businesses within the group, closing eight others, selling property and getting rid of over 700 staff.

> **ATB Laurence Scott is still making electric motors in Norwich, over 125 years after Scott and Paris first came to Norwich**

Help came from an unlikely source when a group of three American businessmen, George Clair, John Lumsden and Dick McEntire, stepped in and after protracted negotiations bought the business for £4.1 million. The deal did not include the Gothic Works which they leased from FKI for three years. Clair and his colleagues envisaged a bright future for LSE, developing a range of high efficiency electric motors to be sold in the US. They made no promises about retaining all the 225 jobs and indicated that they were considering outsourcing manufacturing. The sense of optimism was short-lived as within three years, LSE was again in crisis. Despite a full order book it was suffering from cash flow problems and in May 2007 went into administration. The administrators made 79 redundancies but announced they were hoping to sell the business as a going concern.

STABILITY

This time there were no long drawn out negotiations as LSE was snapped up by the ATB group, a division of Austrian company ATB Austria Antriebstechnik, manufacturers of electric motors. The new business, renamed ATB Laurence Scott, made additional investment at the Gothic Works, installing a new motor test centre at a cost of £2.5 million and, as a sign of confidence in the future, took on three apprentices – the first taken on in five years. In 2009 ATB resolved the uncertainty over the future of the Gothic Works by buying the freehold. ATB Laurence Scott is now owned by the Wolong Holding Group after ATB became insolvent in October 2011. It appears to have a bright future after years of uncertainty and changes of ownership.

ATB Laurence Scott (ATB LS) is still making electric motors in Norwich, over 125 years after Scott and Paris first came to Norwich to help Jeremiah Colman. It is now the only major manufacturer of large bespoke electric motors in the UK. The company provides a complete service from the initial design to the fabrication of the finished motor. Each of the 170 or so high voltage induction and synchronous motors made each year is built to the customer's requirements and thoroughly tested at the Gothic Works before being dispatched. This is essential as many have to perform reliably in harsh conditions such as the offshore oil and gas industries. Over 80% are exported. ATB Laurence Scott has developed motors using a low starting current – particularly useful where space is at a premium and where there are heavy competing demands on power generation such as oil rigs.

The company is also committed to the future. Taking the view that the best way to secure the supply of skilled workers is to train its own, ATB Laurence Scott currently has over 20 apprentices in its 200-strong workforce. Despite its sometimes troubled history, ATB Laurence Scott is a bastion of engineering expertise and a symbol of the city's industrial heritage.

THE NORWICH DRAPERS

From the seventeenth century, and probably earlier, the shops in Norwich attracted customers from near and far. They served almost every conceivable need, but one trade would come to symbolise the importance of Norwich as a centre for shopping – drapery. The city's drapers would become known throughout East Anglia. Curls, Buntings and Chamberlins are still remembered. Many of the city's earliest shops were clustered around the market place and in the streets that led from it, particularly London Street which would become known for its drapers' stores.

Before the emergence of specialist shops most goods were sold from the workshops where they were made, although many of the craftsmen also had stalls on the market. Until the later part of the seventeenth century there appears to have been no clear distinction between retailing and wholesaling. It seems likely that those craftsmen with workshops on the main streets realised the benefits of displaying their goods in a prominent position outside their premises which led to the development of shops as we know them today. An example of a sixteenth-century shop front can be seen in Bedford Street at number 15. The windows would have been unglazed with the goods displayed on a counter in front, which would be pulled up at night to act as a shutter, making the premises secure.

Below:
Buntings at the
corner of St

Stephens St and
Rampant Horse
Street in 1912.

A PROFUSION OF SHOPS

Many of the shops would be familiar today. There were those selling expensive luxuries such as tea, coffee and chocolate. Confectioners sold whole 'sugar loaves' of refined sugar to the wealthy and scrapings of sugar in a screw of paper to the poor. Tobacconists supplied pipe tobacco to rich and poor alike. Haberdashers sold trinkets, nick-knacks and fancy goods – small cheap items not stocked by the larger merchants. The city's well established leather industry supplied the glovers and shoe-makers, whilst china shops sold the china and earthenware for domestic use that was replacing the traditional pewter dishes. There would also have been the apothecary, crammed with bottles and jars holding herbs and patent remedies, many concocted by the apothecary himself.

A trade directory published in 1830 provides evidence of the number and variety of shops. It listed 20 booksellers and stationers (including John Jarrold and Sons – who also sold patent medicines), two cheese factors, 18 china, glass and earthenware dealers, 27 confectioners – some of whom also sold fruit, and more than 70 grocers. There were also 134 described as 'shopkeepers and dealers in sundries', probably the corner shops which were a feature of almost every part of Norwich. The directory also listed 31 linen drapers, 63 milliners and 13 silk mercers. As most people made their own clothes, there was a large demand for the fabrics they sold – many woven locally but others imported from Europe and Asia.

This pattern of small specialist shops was challenged by a new phenomenon which emerged during the 1830s in Britain, France and the United States – the department store. In Britain, drapers such as Charles Harrod in London, and John Watts, who founded Kendals in Manchester, recognised they could increase their business by stocking a wider range of goods. In Norwich, drapers such as the Curl brothers, Arthur Bunting, Richard Garland, Robert Bond and Henry Chamberlin took the same approach. Several of them were closely linked by marriage

and commercial convenience; Arthur Bunting was originally in business with two of the Curl brothers, whilst John Bunting was a director and later Chairman of Chamberlins. Not all of the city's drapery stores followed suit. Some like I. W. Caley in London Street, who proudly advertised their patronage by the royal family, concentrated on drapery alone.

CURL BROTHERS

In the spring of 1902 Curl Brothers opened a splendid new three-story drapery and furniture store on Red Lion Street, adjoining their existing premises on Rampant Horse Street. It had been built quickly; construction had only started the previous October. The new store was a visible symbol of just how far the Curl brothers had come in a short time. Having been trading as wholesale and retail drapers on Rampant Horse Street for less than 20 years, the business now had more than 500 employees.

With its grand entrance, and window displays crammed with goods, the new store brought glamour to Red Lion Street. The frontage was lit by 11 large electric lamps, each of 200 candlepower, which also illuminated the surrounding area. The store was lavishly fitted out; the ladies' and children's departments on the ground floor had light green tinted walls and the mahogany serving counters were embellished by ebony fittings. The space between the existing shop and the new building was utilised to provide ventilation and to accommodate an electric lift which served all floors.

A particular feature was the furnishing arcade with its display of wardrobes, dressing tables, dining tables and cabinets where Curl Brothers sold suites of furniture costing a few pounds and also 'those elaborate sets only to be acquired by those whom fortune had favoured financially' as their catalogue described them. Situated conveniently close by was the carpet showroom with its large display of rugs and carpets.

THE MOURNING SERVICE

One of the more interesting services provided by the store was its Mourning Service for the bereaved. In the firm's spring and summer catalogue of 1900 the Mourning Department announced that 'In addition to the usual Dressmaking and Millinery connected with Mourning Orders, we are in a position to undertake the Entire Management of Funerals.' The firm reassured potential customers that 'Horses, Hearses, Carriages, Bearers etc [are] provided under the personal supervision of a competent man'.

The china, glassware and bedding departments were located in the Rampant Horse Street building along with wallpaper and millinery. The majority of the women's clothes sold were made to measure, sewn by the scores of seamstresses who worked in the old building, close to the fitting and retiring rooms. Men's and boy's clothes, manufactured at the firm's Norwich Pottergate factory, were sold in the store, and supplied through the firm's wholesale department to shops across the United Kingdom. The Pottergate factory was on the south side of the road, between Fishers Lane and Cow Hill and may have been the former premises of Willet Nephew and Company. The factory survived the First World War but had closed by 1924.

Left: Henley Curl, co-owner of the Curl Brothers drapery, which opened its three-storey premises in 1902.

The three Curl brothers, Edward, Jacob and Henley, had arrived in Norwich in the late 1850s. The family were originally from the East Winch area of West Norfolk although their father Joseph had been a shopkeeper in South Norfolk, and later in West Winch before coming to live in Norwich. He was later described in census returns as a 'Proprietor of Houses', i.e. someone who lived off the income from his properties, and as a 'Gentleman'.

By 1861, Edward and Jacob were working as assistant drapers at Henry Snowdon's large store in St Georges Bridge Street, where Bunting, Snowdon's brother-in-law, was an apprentice. Jacob went on to establish himself as a draper in St Benedicts Street, on the north side close to St Swithin's Church. In 1866, Edward went into partnership with Arthur Bunting, opening a wholesale and retail drapers' shop at the corner of St Stephens Street and Rampant Horse Street. Henley Curl later joined them, having worked for a time as a shopman in John Snowdon's drapery shop in the market place. Edward Curl left the business in July 1880. The partnership continued for a further two years before being dissolved in October 1882 when Bunting continued to run the St Stephens Street shop.

CONVERSION OF THE RAMPANT HORSE HOTEL

Henley Curl and Arthur Bunting had acquired the Rampant Horse Hotel, an old coaching inn, in 1879, perhaps intending to expand their business there. But in 1883 the three Curl brothers converted the inn into a wholesale and retail draper's shop, using the former hotel billiard room as a showroom for men's and boys' clothing. The hotel yard, which ran through to Orford Place was covered over and electric lighting installed to provide additional display space. The former hotel cellars were extended and used for storage – there were separate rooms for Manchester cotton goods, flannel, blankets, Worsted cloth and Berlin goods.

At the Orford Place entrance there was an enquiry office for the wholesale trade with a board listing the whereabouts of the company's commercial travellers.

Over the next few years the brothers acquired adjoining properties in Rampant Horse Street and Red Lion Street. Reportedly, this involved the closure of four public houses. By the late 1890s Curl Brothers employed over 200 staff, some of whom lived on the top floor of the Rampant Horse Street store or in a large house on Castle Meadow owned by the brothers. The house was near Opie Street and accommodated more than 20 female staff, the majority of whom were under 21 and came from outside Norwich. Great attention was paid to customer service and new staff were not permitted to speak to customers during their first two years at the shop whilst being trained. Branches of Curl Brothers were opened at Lowestoft and Harleston, and in Norwich on Magdalen Road at the corner of Stacy Road, and on Ber Street. They also continued to trade from Jacob Curl's premises in St Benedicts Street.

Sadly, by the time the new shop on Red Lion Street opened, only one of the three brothers was alive to see it. Edward, who seems to have suffered from ill-health and had retired from the business before reaching his 50th birthday, died in October 1894. He was followed within six months by Jacob, who died suddenly at his Ipswich Road home in the early hours of Friday 5th April 1895. Henley Curl was joined in the business by his sons Harry and Percy, and Jacob's son Ernest. This quartet would run the business for the next 25 years and formed the board of directors when Curl Brothers became a limited company in 1899.

Under their direction, Curl Brothers continued to flourish and by the Christmas season of 1925 claimed 'practically everything can be had that has to do with the clothing of the person or the furnishing of the home' at their store. Although holding a large range of non-drapery items, it was the drapery department that provided 'all that the heart could desire in the way of

Christmas presents – including fashionable dresses, smart hosiery, and in the underwear department, all the latest and daintiest things in nightgowns, camisoles, silk evening petticoats etc'. The store also stocked a multitude of fancy goods including cushions and cosies, all kinds of bead chains, manicure sets, wallets, purses and metal wares.

THE DRAPERY AND GENERAL INVESTMENT TRUST

In view of the company's continuing success it came as some surprise when it emerged in December 1925 that Curl Brothers had been acquired by the Drapery and General Investment Trust. The Trust was a holding company established to buy up drapery and department stores in England. It had already acquired several stores in London, Yorkshire, Glasgow and on the south coast. One of the Curl Brothers' directors commented in the local press that 'the local management will not be interfered with' and that 'the present directors [will] remain in office'. He also indicated that the directors would themselves be buying shares in the new trust. Two years later the Drapery Trust itself was effectively taken over by Debenhams, a manufacturer and wholesaler of clothing with interests in the UK and abroad. They already owned Marshall and Snelgrove and Harvey Nicholls in London and were hoping to expand.

By then the surviving founder had died. Henley Curl died in January 1926 aged 87 at home on Unthank Road. Although he had relinquished responsibility for the management of the business, he still took an interest and had visited the store only a few days before his death. He was the only one of the three brothers to become involved in local politics – having been a Liberal councillor for the ward where the store stood for many years, and had resigned as an Alderman only four years prior to his death.

Although owned by Debenhams, Percy and Harry Curl continued to manage Curl Brothers – Percy being responsible for the retail side

Left: Curl's Red Lion Street site in 1952, awaiting rebuilding.

whilst Harry managed the wholesale business. Despite the economic difficulties of the inter-war period which affected Norwich as it did the rest of the United Kingdom, Curl's store continued to be an important port of call for shoppers. This was brought to an abrupt end in late April 1941 when the store was completely destroyed in the heaviest air raid of the war in Norwich. When the rubble had been cleared part of the site was converted into a large static water tank, available to assist firefighting in the event of further raids, and later used as a car park prior to post-war rebuilding. Following the raid Debenhams acted quickly to secure alternative premises. A shop in Exchange Street adjoining the Post Office Tavern was acquired to house the furniture department whilst the all-important women's fashions department moved to Westlegate. At about the same time Debenhams bought Garland's London Street store.

THE NEW STORE

It would be more than a decade before Curls had a flagship store on Red Lion Street. But when it did it was bigger and better than before. Opened in the spring of 1956, the new store had 70,000 square feet of display space on four floors and accommodation for 400 staff. It was air-conditioned and its escalators,

the first in East Anglia, were claimed to be four times safer than stairs. The new store was well situated with entrances on four of the city's central streets, close to the bus station and passed by most of the city bus routes. The opening ceremony was performed by Percy Curl in April in front of a crowd of over 300 eager customers. Once the store opened additional tills had to be installed to cope with the rush of business. Percy and Harry Curl had withdrawn from the management of the firm in 1952 and Harry died later that same year. Percy lived for another seven years, long enough to see the new store rise from the ashes.

The four well-stocked floors carried a tempting array of goods. In the basement were kitchenware, ironmongery, household gadgets, garden furniture, linen, china, glass, electrical appliances and wallpaper, with staff on hand to demonstrate the appliances. On the ground floor was men's and boys' wear, soft furnishings, perfume and jewellery, whilst women's fashion, children's wear and baby linen occupied the first floor. Furniture was on the second floor, much of it displayed in room settings to show just how it would look in customers' homes.

In a brochure issued to celebrate the new store, the company described its potential customers as farmers and their wives and the many men and women who worked in the city's industries – including the 10,000 footwear workers, the thousands employed at nearby Norwich Union, and those working in engineering, chocolate, cracker making and brewing. It reflected a city with employment patterns much different to those of today.

Staff working hours were 9 a.m. – 5.30 p.m., 5 days a week, and 9 a.m. – 1 p.m. on Thursday, which was early closing day. There was an hour for lunch along with two short breaks during the working day. After being with the firm for six months all staff were entitled to two weeks' paid leave, which increased to three weeks after ten years' service. They were also entitled to a ten percent staff discount on goods bought in the store. As part of the store's training programme, staff were encouraged to take the Junior or Senior Retail Certificate by attending Norwich City College for one morning a week.

Now renamed Debenhams, the Orford Place store continues to be one of Norwich's major stores.

BUNTINGS

Following the dissolution of his partnership with Henley Curl in 1882, Arthur Bunting continued the business under his own name at St Stephen's corner, later expanding by taking in adjoining properties on St Stephens Street and along Rampant Horse Street.

Trading under the slogan 'Latest, Cheapest, Best', Buntings catered almost solely for women, and advertised in 1909 that they laid before what they described as their fair patrons 'the very latest modes in costumes, millinery and accessories, together with the most artistic and serviceable furniture and fabrics for domestic use', and all at reasonable prices. The pride of the store was the mantel and dress department which provided well-cut ready-made evening gowns, coats, costumes and travelling wear. For those customers who preferred to have their clothes made to

measure, the store had its own dressmaking department. To make the customer's outfits complete the Lace department carried a comprehensive assortment of collars, yokes, frills, ruffles and 'more varieties of dainty trifles than we could well enumerate.' The millinery showroom had a collection of 'Parisian' hats.

RULES AND REGULATIONS FOR THE STAFF

The store employed a large number of staff. Most began work at 8.20 a.m. although the 'dusters' and the male apprentices had to be there by 7.45 a.m. to get ready for opening. Customers would be greeted at the door and escorted to a counter by a floor walker where they would be served. The male staff wore black coats and waistcoats and were not permitted to remove their coats when serving customers or to ask a customer to move to another counter without the permission of the floor walker or at the customer's express request. The female staff wore black stuff dresses.

No employee was permitted to leave the shop in the evening before the shop walker had declared the shop closed. Each employee was issued with a book of 97 rules and regulations which they were encouraged to memorise. The rules covered almost all aspects of personal behaviour and how business in the store should be conducted. Breaches were subject to fines and in the case of anybody caught smoking in the staff bedrooms, by dismissal. The census of 1891 recorded 20 employees living there, mainly draper's assistants and apprentices, one of whom was John Bunting, the nephew of the proprietor. They were cared for by a housekeeper and three domestic servants. The rules extended to the living accommodation. All had to be in their rooms by 10.30 each evening. There was no escape on the Sabbath as every apprentice was expected to attend church at least once.

A feature of Buntings was the Liberty room where a selection of the London firm's cushion squares, table covers, carpets, curtains and bric-a-brac was displayed in a rather crowded showroom. Adjoining it was a tea-room. By the early years of the twentieth century the store had a large furniture department where carpets, rugs and curtains could also be obtained. Buntings had also developed a substantial mail-order business – supplying its customers who lived outside Norwich with catalogues so they could shop by post.

ARTHUR BUNTING

Born and brought up in Norwich where his father was a plumber and glazier in St Giles, Arthur Bunting never married. With no children of his own, Arthur brought two of his nephews into the business. John Walter Bunting was the first, apprenticed to the firm during the early 1890s when in his early teens. His brother Charles joined the firm in 1898, having been apprenticed in London. During his later years Arthur lived in style at The Grange in Old Catton, sharing it with his nieces Kate and Ellen Snowdon and employing four servants and a coachman. John W. Bunting would marry Kate Snowdon in July 1903.

The brothers soon had to take on the responsibility of managing the business, following the death of their uncle in 1905. Upon returning from a visit to London, Arthur Bunting was taken ill with a chill which subsequently developed into bronchial pneumonia. He died on the morning of the 11th May at his Old Catton house aged 61, leaving effects valued at over £86,000. Charles took over as Managing Director and John became a director, although the business continued to be known as Arthur Bunting and Company. John Bunting also became a director of Chamberlin and Company. Since arriving in Norwich, he had become a close personal friend of Sir George Chamberlin and upon Chamberlin's death in 1928 became Chairman and Managing Director of the firm.

In 1912 the store was completely rebuilt. Designed by A. F. Scott and built of reinforced concrete, with a stone façade divided into bays above ground floor level, it brought a sense of grandeur to St Stephen's corner. It was topped off by the cupola attic storey above the corner entrance. By the mid-1920s Bunting's store was a major attraction for women shoppers, having extended the range of goods stocked. On the lower ground floor was a display of suitcases, handbags, needle cases, tea cosies, work boxes, fountain pens and what were intriguingly described as 'ebony, tortoiseshell and silver requisites'.

Far left: Charles Arthur Bunting.
Left: John Walter Bunting.

Caley's crackers were sold at Christmas time. Hosiery, gloves, ties, scarves, pyjamas, travelling rugs and silks were displayed on the ground floor. Women's fashions occupied the first floor where the prices of dresses ranged from 29 shillings to 12 guineas. China and glassware, including Chippendale reproductions, shared the second floor with the shoe department – which stocked Russian boots at 25 shillings a pair. Customers were welcomed by a commissionaire, resplendent in a blue uniform, complete with gold braid and brass buttons, before being met by the formally dressed floor walker. The store also had a fine restaurant where customers could enjoy their meal to a background of orchestral music.

Like other city centre shops, Buntings suffered from war-time air raids and was damaged during the April 1941 raids that destroyed Curls. Service to customers resumed on the ground floor but the upper part of the building was taken over for use as a NAFFI club for service personnel. By now, Charles Bunting was running the business, John having died, aged only 59, in November 1934 after an unsuccessful operation.

THE MOVE FROM 'BUNTING'S CORNER'

In 1948, Marks and Spencer, looking for premises for a Norwich store, bought the St Stephens site, paying what was said at the time to be the highest price ever paid for a commercial property in Norwich. After extensive conversion, the new M&S store opened in March 1950. By then Buntings had been acquired by Debenhams, who rehoused the business in the recently bought shop of house furnishers Goodways, next door to Garlands in London Street. It remained a separate shop until 1963 when it became part of Garlands.

Charles Bunting died aged 72 in July 1950 at his home at Drayton. In addition to being the Managing Director of Buntings he had been a director of Fras Hinde and Co the silk weavers. In his private life he was an assiduous and knowledgeable collector of antique silver and furniture and owned several paintings by the Norfolk artist Alfred Munnings.

GARLANDS

Like the Curl brothers before him, Richard Ellary Garland came to Norwich to make his way. The son of a draper in Stroud in Gloucestershire, he was privately educated there and at Tewkesbury, before serving an apprenticeship in his father's trade near London. He then traded as a draper for a short time at Bexley in Kent.

In the spring of 1862 he bought William Piper's drapery business at 17 London Street, Norwich. He was entering a very competitive trade – the city had almost 50 other draper's shops with seven in London Street alone. Norwich's rapidly growing population provided a large market for women's clothes.

Within weeks of taking over the shop, Garland was inviting ladies to visit a private room where they could view ready-made linens and a great variety of home-made skirts. By March 1871, the shop was employing 20 assistants, nearly all female, several of whom, including one of the dressmakers, lived over the London Street shop.

The practice of drapers providing accommodation for their staff continued well into the late 1930s. The store not only sold ready-made and bespoke women's clothes but also supplied thousands of yards of dress fabrics as well as sheeting, flannel and lace curtains.

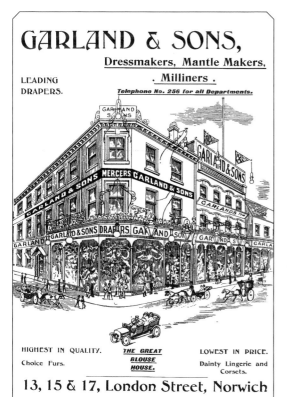

GARLAND & SONS,

Dressmakers, Mantle Makers,

. Milliners .

LEADING DRAPERS.

Telephone No. 256 for all Departments.

HIGHEST IN QUALITY.   THE GREAT BLOUSE HOUSE.   LOWEST IN PRICE.
Choice Furs.   Dainty Lingerie and Corsets.

13, 15 & 17, London Street, Norwich

In the 1860s the city had almost 50 draper's shops, with seven in London Street alone.

Opposite: Bomb damage at Buntings. Left: 1910 advertisement for Garlands. Right: Richard Garland.

By 1880 Garland had also acquired the adjoining shop at 15 London Street and a few years later would expand further by buying English's drapers at number 13. He was establishing a reputation for the quality of the calico he sold and for gloves. At one time the shop was known as the Norwich Glove House. Richard Garland no longer lived above the shop but had moved to St Georges Middle Street, close to Alms Lane, and later moved to Unthank Road. Unlike many of his contemporaries he took little part in public life but devoted his considerable energies to making a success of his business. In his private life he was a member of the Princes Street Congregational Church. In the late 1880s Richard's two sons, Frank and Henry joined the business. Frank had been apprenticed to Roberts of Islington, a large north London department store, before coming to work with his father in 1886.

> **By the mid-1920s, Garland's store had 27 departments catering for men, women and children.**

Left: Frank Garland. Opposite, left to right: Garland's London Street store decorated for the Silver Jubilee in 1935; Advertisement after Garland's 1930 re-opening.

NOVELTIES FROM LONDON, PARIS AND BERLIN

Garlands was selling calico, gloves, serge at eleven pence halfpenny a yard, white Turkish towels at four for eight pence halfpenny and advertising that the shop held 'a new stock of distinguished novelties from London, Paris and Berlin'. This included notepaper, candlesticks, straw table mats, pincushions, flowerpots, books at sixpence halfpenny each, gramophones at 16 shillings and 9 pence and records at 2 shillings. Customers who spent £1 or more were offered a glass of port wine!

Soon after the turn of the century the family suffered two heavy blows in quick succession. Henry Garland died in October 1909 after a long illness and his father Richard the following August. At the time of his death at the age of 73, Richard Garland was reputed to be the oldest active businessman in Norwich, having spent almost half a century trading in London Street.

Frank Garland was now responsible for managing the firm, until his sons Neville and Cyril became directors in the 1920s. He continued the drapery trade tradition of providing accommodation for staff at his home in St Helen's House in Bishopgate. Just prior to the First World War there were 21 female shop assistants living at the house, all but one were single and in their late teens or twenties. Most came from Norfolk and Suffolk with a few from further afield. The youngest was Kathleen Barker – a 16 year old apprentice from Hoxne in Suffolk.

By the mid-1920s, Garland's store, now spread along London Street, had 27 departments catering for men, women and children. An advertising feature of the time described the toy department in glowing terms, 'The toy bazaar overflows with children's "heart's delights". There are toys of every description, dolls of all kinds and sizes, Teddy bears, furry dogs, cats, rabbits etc. Trains on rails appear to be a speciality at Garlands'. There was also a grotto with a difference featuring old Mother Hubbard – the scenery painted by one of the staff at the Maddermarket Theatre. Children were taken round by Father Christmas but received their present from Mother Hubbard when they knocked on the door of her red brick house.

REBUILDING

In 1929 the adjoining draper's shop of Masters Godfrey and Co at number 19 was acquired and incorporated into the store as part of a major rebuilding project. The new store was opened on Tuesday 25th March 1930 by the Lady Mayoress, who witnessed a parade of mannequins wearing English costumes, supplied by the Maddermarket Theatre, covering the period from the Norman Conquest to the founding of the firm in 1862. The new building was described as a good example of the best type of modern drapery store, complete with an entrance arcade and designed to provide the largest amount of display space. Upon entering, the customer was provided with a complete view of the ground floor drapery department, including a new needlework department.

The first floor held the fashion department and, like the ground floor, was lit by natural light from ceiling lights. Once they had completed their shopping, customers could retire to the second-floor restaurant for refreshment and food. The second floor also held the workrooms where Garland's seamstresses worked.

Frank Garland retired from active management in 1936 but continued as Chairman of the company until it was bought by Debenhams in 1942.

The post-war period saw further improvements. In 1960 a new sales floor was installed and in 1962 a 'Young Fashions' shop aimed at teenage girls was opened on the first floor. There was a major setback in 1970 when the store was almost completely destroyed by fire. Late in the afternoon of Saturday 1st August, a chip pan caught fire and spread rapidly through ducting. When firemen first arrived they discovered staff still serving customers, oblivious of the fire, and ordered an immediate evacuation. Within 30 minutes the first floor was well ablaze and by 8 p.m. the fire had burnt through the London Street frontage and the roof had collapsed. It took the efforts of 70 firemen over three hours to get the fire under control. They prevented it spreading to neighbouring buildings, stopping a major conflagration in the crowded London Street shopping area. The cost of the damage was estimated at over £1 million, being described as Norwich's most disastrous fire since the Blitz.

The store was soon rebuilt and reopened by the designer Hardy Amies in October 1973, who described it as 'really above anything I have seen.' The new store had 46,000 square feet of shopping space devoted to fashion and accessories. It also featured 'shops within shops' where well-known names included Russell and Bromley, Jaeger, and Berketex, and a restaurant. The first customer on the opening day, a woman from West Earlham in Norwich, received a bouquet of flowers and was allowed to select goods to the value of £30 from the store without charge.

After such a major investment it came as a shock when Debenhams announced in January 1984 that Garlands would be closing as part of a rationalisation process. Norwich was the only place outside London where Debenhams had two stores. They had decided to close Garlands and renovate the Red Lion Street store where, although there would be no more actual space, there would be a 'completely new environment and concept' with some of Garlands more popular individual departments moving there. Over 100 staff were offered jobs elsewhere by Debenhams. The building was later sold to a developer linked to Debenhams for conversion to individual shops units.

Left: After the fire at Garlands in 1970. Opposite: Bond's Ber Street store (second building from the left) in 1936.

BONDS

Although Bonds of All Saints Green and Ber Street would become one of Norwich's most fashionable department stores, its beginnings were far from propitious. In March 1879, Robert Hearne Bond took over a small draper's shop in Ber Street, remote from the main shopping area. At the time there were five drapers in Ber Street alone, including a branch of Curl Brothers a few doors down. The early years must have been difficult but by the time of his death Robert Bond had turned his small shop into one of the city's major drapers.

Robert Hearne Bond was brought up by his mother, Ann, after the death of his father (Ludham farmer George Bond) when Robert was only three years old. Ann not only raised a large family but continued to farm over 100 acres of arable and marsh land at Hall Common Farm near Ludham.

Having worked as a grocer's assistant in London, by the early 1870s Robert was employed as a 'draper's foreman' at Moulsham Street, Chelmsford. It seems probable he was working for his older brother John who was a draper in the town with shops at Moulsham Street and the High Street. In March 1879,

having married Mary Owen and started a family, he returned to Norfolk where he bought Randall Woodland's draper's, hosier's and haberdasher's shop at number 19 Ber Street. The shop was located on the south side of Ber Street about halfway between Thorn Lane and the city end of the street.

CHEAP DRAPERY

He wasted no time, placing a large advertisement on the front page of the Norwich Mercury announcing a 'Great Sale of Drapery', offering the entire stock he had purchased from Woodland at considerably less than half price. Two weeks later a further advert offered 'Cheap Drapery' with prices commencing at one penny, three farthings and 'A Quantity of Hats and Fancy goods almost given away'. His efforts appear to have been successful as by the end of April, under the banner 'Cheap Drapery, Cheap Drapery', Bond was advertising his new stock of spring goods, 'Which will be found the cheapest in the city', and drawing attention to his large stock of trimmed hats and bonnets. The shop offered no credit – everything had to be paid for in cash – 'Ready Money Only'.

When the second anniversary of the business came round Robert and Mary Bond were sharing their home above the shop with two assistants, two draper's apprentices and a milliner's assistant. Mary Bond is credited with building up the millinery business for which the store would become renowned. The success of the business enabled Robert Bond to expand. In 1895 he bought the adjacent public house, the Jubilee Tavern, at number 21 and a few years later acquired Thomas Avery's grocer's shop at number 15.

For a time during the 1890s Bond had a second shop in St Georges Bridge Street (now St Georges Street) near the junction with Colegate. It was short-lived and had been disposed of by 1904. By then the family had moved to All Saints Green, occupying a house on the west side of the road formerly owned by Francis Hinde, the silk manufacturer. The store also had a presence on All Saints Green, having opened a shop at number 17 which would later be linked to the Ber Street shop by an arcade.

By this time two of Robert and Mary's sons had joined the business, William in 1897 and Ernest in 1903. As was customary, they had been trained elsewhere; William at the millinery and fancy goods business run by Julia Hardy in the Buttermarket at Bury St Edmunds, and Ernest with a draper in Bedford. Both would serve the firm for many years – William would succeed his father as Chairman, followed by Ernest, whose service was only interrupted by his time in the army during the First World War. A third son, John Owen Bond, became an architect and his practice would be responsible for the 1938 extension to the store, as well as the Haymarket and Carlton cinemas. Robert Hearne Bond died in 1924, much mourned. His funeral service took place at the church of St Michael at Thorn, close to his store, where he had worshipped for many years.

THE THATCHED CINEMA

The 1920s and 30s saw Bonds as one of the city's major stores. In 1930 the company acquired the former Thatched Cinema on All Saints Green which was converted for use as a restaurant, conference hall and offices. The millinery department was a particular feature of the store – during this period there were 20 milliners busy making hats, 30 sales assistants selling them, and it was claimed the store sold 1,000 hats on a Saturday. Much attention was paid to training the staff. Joyce Gurney-Read recorded that 'It was the custom for staff to serve a three year apprenticeship, and in most cases pay for

R. H. BOND,
15-17-19-21-23, BER STREET, NORWICH,

CASH DRAPER,

Has the Largest Stock of **Millinery** in the Eastern Counties.

A SECTION OF MILLINERY SHOWROOMS.   BLOUSE & UNDERCLOTHING DEPARTMENT.

Departments :

Millinery	Lace	Blouse Materials	Furs
Blouse	Mantles	Gloves	Ribbons
Dress	Underclothing	Children's Outfitting	Hosiery

The Public are heartily invited to inspect our Extensive SHOWROOMS.

DRESS DEPARTMENT.   MANTLE & COSTUME SHOWROOM.

Household Linen. ——— Furnishing.

An Immense Variety of Goods in all Departments.
AT THE LOWEST CASH PRICES.

Far left: Advertisement for Bond's cash drapers in 1910. Left: Robert Herne Bond.

the privilege, but Ernest was against this, so apprentices were paid 6s. per week plus lunches.'

Their first year was spent packing and unpacking, disentangling string, smoothing out tissue paper, picking up pins, and brushing and dusting the vast departmental displays. After three years they were promoted to 'improvers' and were then occasionally allowed to serve if all the sales staff were busy. All fashion garments carried a 'Bonds' label which had to be sewn in. This was one of the 'improvers' jobs, as well as going through all stock to ensure that buttons were secure.

In 1938 the premises at 23 to 25 All Saints Green, next door to the Thatched Cinema, became available and a new showroom was built. Medieval in appearance, it was intended to complement the style of the Thatched Cinema. By this time the store employed over 200 people. In addition to William and Ernest, a third generation of the Bond family had become involved in running the business. Ernest's sister Ida Bond, and his son, Richard, joined the firm along with Eric Hinde, his son-in-law.

Like Curls and Buntings, Bonds suffered severe wartime damage. In the early morning of 27th June 1942, All Saints Green was heavily bombed and the store and the Thatched Cinema completely burnt out. Bonds was nothing if not resilient and the shop was soon trading again. Within three days clothes were being sold from several buses parked on the store car park. The offices were relocated to a building on the opposite side of All Saints Green, and a restaurant opened in a tin hut on the car park. The restaurant was later relocated to St Catherines Close a few hundred yards away. More permanent accommodation was soon found. A shop on Thorpe Road, close to the junction with Rosary Road was found for the carpet and furniture departments whilst the other departments moved into a building on Red Lion Street, which is currently occupied by a bank. In December 1944 the business suffered a personal blow when William Bond died suddenly whilst at the store. He was 70 but still actively involved.

THE CITY'S FIRST MODERN DEPARTMENT STORE

In 1946 rebuilding began. Robert Owen Bond, grandson of the founder and now working in his father's architectural practice, designed the sweeping three-story neo-Georgian store that still dominates the junction of Ber Street and All Saints Green. It took nearly five years to complete but it gave the city its first modern department store. The 1950s and 1960s were good for Bonds. It was a time of increasing prosperity as Britain recovered from the war and domestic goods became more readily available and affordable. The business had moved away from Robert Bond's emphasis on 'Cheap Drapery'. Having decided it could not compete at the bottom of the market, it now concentrated on selling top quality merchandise and providing good service. The store was still recognisably a drapers. Most of the goods featured in an advertisement for the January sale of 1960 were women's clothes, linen and bedding, some men's wear and items of haberdashery such as tablecloths and oven gloves. Hats were featured prominently with 1,000 available at bargain prices ranging from five to 20 shillings. In a sign of things to come, the sale included three new Adamatic combined washing machine/spin driers at £70 each. How much of a bargain they were is debatable as the advert made it clear they were shop soiled demonstration models.

A men's clothing department was added when Greens in the Haymarket closed in 1960, its stock and goodwill moving to Bonds. Two years later, Cluttens of East Dereham, a women's fashion store, was purchased and modernised with a further 2,000 square feet of space being added. The death of Ernest Bond in February 1963 at the age of 83 was the end of an era. Born above his father's shop in the year the business was founded, he remained Chairman until his death. Outside the firm his interests had been mainly sporting, and he had been a director of Norwich City Football Club for many years.

To all appearances Bonds approached its centenary in 1979 with confidence. It was one of the city's only two family owned department stores – Jarrolds being the other – and had recently finished a massive redevelopment. The year before over £1 million had been spent adding 14,000 square feet of selling space to give 96,000 in total. The new two-storey extension housed the confectionery and stationery departments and flower shop. On the second floor was a hairdressing and beauty salon, run by Glemby International, a US firm said to be the largest in-store hairdressing organisation in the world. On the first floor was a new restaurant with space for 160 diners.

The store now had 70 departments and there were plans for further improvements, including a new furniture showroom and a large fabric and haberdashery department on the ground floor. But the expansion had been costly and the then Managing Director, Nicholas Hinde, hinted at the strain on the company's finances when he commented that it was a large investment for a privately owned business and referred to the difficulties in running such a business. At the time all but one of the directors were members of the Bond family. These difficulties became public three years later when Hinde resigned after what was reported as a boardroom split.

JOHN LEWIS

Within weeks Bonds had been sold. On Monday 24th May 1982 the store closed ten minutes early and the 300 staff were informed the store had been bought by the John Lewis Partnership The new owners promised there would be no redundancies. The price was reported to be less than £5 million. Some light was shed on the reason for the sale a few days later when the financial position of Bonds became public. The business had made a loss of £297,000 the previous year, three times that of 1980, and its last profitable year had been 1978.

The losses were largely attributed to the cost of the redevelopment and underlined the difficulties faced by provincial stores in funding modernisation and expansion. The John Lewis Partnership had those resources and within two years announced plans to double the floor space and build a new multi-storey car park next to the store. Renamed as John Lewis in 2001, the All Saints Green store continues to be one of Norwich's favoured destinations for shoppers, but for many older people it will always be Bonds.

Although the major drapers dominated the trade in Norwich there were other smaller firms, such as Henry Jarvis and Sons, and Butchers in Bedford Street.

HENRY JARVIS

Jarvis's opened in 1908 in St Benedicts Street, close to the church of St Swithin, and soon expanded after buying and demolishing several cottages in St Swithins Alley. Just before the Second World War further expansion took place when an imposing arcade entrance was added. The store was destroyed by wartime bombing but rebuilt in 1950. It was extended further during the next decade and by the time the firm celebrated its 60th birthday in 1968, the St Benedicts shop was a medium-sized department store. It covered three floors, employed 120 staff, with car parking for 100 customers' cars, and had recently added a new carpet department, a lingerie section and a coffee bar. It was a family business run by brothers Leonard, Frank and Edward Jarvis, and Frank's son David. In 1973 the firm received an offer from a property developers described as being too good to turn down and the store closed its doors on Christmas Eve that year.

BUTCHERS

When it closed, Butchers was the last of the Norwich drapers. It combined the sale of soft furnishings and fabrics with a traditional haberdashery that stocked everything from pins to dusters. The firm traded from a building at the corner of Swan Lane and Bedford Street which until 1859 had been a public house. It then became a genteel drapers and milliners run by the Plummer sisters who sold it to George Diggens, a draper, who owned premises on either side of Bedford Street.

In 1909 Diggens leased the building to George Butcher, a draper from Diss, for £250 a year. The top floor accommodated his young family, several of his shop assistants and the family's three servants, whilst Butcher traded from the ground floor. His success enabled him to buy the building in 1920 and it remained in family hands thereafter.

At that time the shop was purely a drapers but George was ambitious. In 1930 a basement was excavated to provide more selling space and later the two top floors were brought into use. Now managed by George's sons Leslie, Harold and Stanley, Butchers expanded in the post-war period, buying the nearby Hovells basket shop in 1970, and, a few years later, Loads of North Walsham, a well-established drapers. George had died in 1961.

The Bedford Street building remained much as it had been since the nineteenth century until it was refurbished in 1980. It remained a general drapery until further refurbishment in 1988/9 when the ground floor windows were given a more graceful appearance and new corporate colours of ultramarine blue, coral pink and grey adopted. At the same time the sales floors were brought up to date and a decision was made to discontinue men's and women's fashions and concentrate on general drapery. The building continues as a general drapers but no longer under the Butcher name.

TODAY

There are still visible reminders of the great Norwich drapers; Debenhams continues to trade from the Curls building, the Buntings building still stands at the corner of St Stephens and Rampant Horse Street, and John Lewis are still based at the All Saints Green store built for Bonds in 1946. But perhaps the most poignant reminder is the great red brick building on Guildhall Hill which formerly housed Chamberlins, the grandest of the city's drapers and the subject of the following case study.

Right: Butcher's shop in Bedford Street in 2000.

CHAMBERLINS

At about 4 a.m. on Monday 1st August 1898, a couple walking home along Dove Street smelt burning, saw hot tar running from Hurn's workshop and raised the alarm. They had good cause to be concerned. Hurns made ropes, sails and wagon covers and used tar and other highly inflammable materials. Despite the strenuous efforts of the city's fire brigade, assisted by firemen from Carrow works and the Anchor Brewery, the fire spread and in a few hours had destroyed not only Hurns but the rear part of Chamberlin's store, including the attractive galleried well which held the wholesale haberdashery and dress business, doing damage estimated at £80,000. The adjacent public library was also badly damaged with much of the stock affected by smoke and water. There was no loss of life. Several of Chamberlin's staff who lived above the store were able to escape with their possessions, taking refuge at the Guildhall.

It was a huge blow to the city's largest and most palatial store whose premises dominated the southern end of the market place. Chamberlins reacted swiftly, placing a large notice in the following day's *Eastern Daily Press*. Headed 'The Great Fire of Norwich'. It reassured customers that 'the front portion of our retail premises and the whole of our carpet and furnishing department have been saved from destruction.....the latter and our cash drapery stores will be opened for business today' and 'We hope to have the saved remainder of our premises ready for business in a day or two'.

The fire could have been disastrous but it turned out to be an opportunity for renewal. Within three years the rear of the store had been

Above:
Chamberlin's
Guildhall store
circa 1969.

rebuilt and the interior extensively refurbished. It reopened on Saturday 1st June 1901 with customers being serenaded in the silk saloon by Herr Karoly Kaly's Blue Hungarian Band. The new store was enthusiastically described in the local press as 'one of the finest business establishments in the kingdom. Everywhere are to be seen long lofty rooms, all admirably lighted'. It went on to say 'Upon entering the main doorway the visitor finds on his left the ladies' underclothing and children's department, and on his right the gentleman's department, while immediately in front is the glory of the whole establishment – an immense saloon filled with the most beautiful goods known to the trade, and displayed with a taste that cannot fail to attract the interested attention of ladies'. However, the most striking feature of the refurbishment was the large stained glass window at the end of the saloon containing pictures of Henry Chamberlin senior and his son, Robert, flanked by views of ancient city buildings, the arms of the city, and those of the Chamberlin family. A waiting and reception room for women customers, with fitting rooms and other facilities completed the amenities.

Other improvements included the extension of the Little Bonnet Box where ladies' millinery was on display, and the linking of the main store to the furnishing department on the west side of Library Court by means of a passage. The furnishing department contained 'one of the largest assortments of carpets, linoleums, floor cloths and furniture of every description to be found in the Eastern Counties'. The exterior was not neglected. Large display windows were inserted on the Dove Street aspect of the rebuilt store. There were two entrances facing the market place, with the main one, which was surmounted by an elaborate iron canopy, at the corner of Dove Street, where customers were greeted by a uniformed commissionaire. Chamberlins now extended from Dove Street, round the corner into the market place and up Guildhall Hill to Labour in Vain Yard. Only the ground floor was used for selling – the upper floors housed the counting house and the wholesale department and the basement

stored the heavier wholesale goods. Chamberlins was at the height of its success, and somewhat boastfully claimed in their advertising that Norwich was the city of the Three Cs – Cathedral, Castle and Chamberlins.

THE FOUNDER

The business had been founded by Henry Chamberlin. Born in Norfolk, he had lived at Thorpe-next-Norwich, where he married his first wife Esther, and later at Gresham where he married Sarah Camplin, his second wife. In 1815 he opened a linen draper's shop on the market place at the junction of Guildhall Hill and Dove Lane. Within 15 years he was described as a linen draper, carpet dealer and hat dealer and two of his sons, Henry and Robert, had joined him in the business.

It appears that Robert began taking an active role about 1823, after a period as a draper in Lowestoft. He would be largely responsible for the growth of the business following his father's retirement in the 1840s. Henry senior died in March 1848 aged 75 at his Newmarket Road home. Henry junior left Norwich, taking up residence at Narborough Hall before his sudden death in 1857 when on a visit to King's Lynn.

Robert Chamberlin expanded the modest draper's shop at the corner of Dove Street, buying Coleman's adjoining draper's shop on Guildhall Hill to obtain a large frontage facing the market place and subsequently adding the buildings on the west side of Library Court. By 1869 the current imposing four-story red brick building had been completed. He died in July 1876, his obituary accurately describing him as the proprietor of the 'leading mercantile establishment of the city'. He also took an active part in civic life, having been Sheriff in 1848, and Mayor on three occasions, in 1854, 1856 and 1871, and was described as having a conciliatory disposition and an unobtrusive manner. Robert lived in some style at Catton House outside Norwich which was his home for most of his life and where he raised a large family. His two marriages produced seventeen children, two of

Above, from top: Part of the showroom and the drapery department at Guildhall Hill in 1910. Below: The Botolph Street factory in 1910.

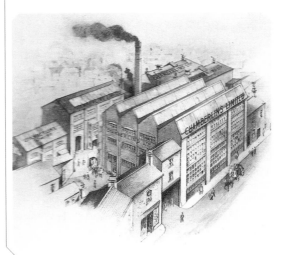

whom, Alexander and George, joined the family business whilst Robert's second son Edward Henry became an officer in the Rifle Brigade and served with distinction in the Indian Mutiny. Robert Chamberlin's estate, valued at around £120,000, was divided between his second wife Ann and his two surviving sons, with Alexander also being left the freehold premises on Guildhall Hill. Alexander, the older of the two brothers by ten years, managed the finances whilst George became Managing Director.

THE CITY'S MOST PALATIAL STORE

As the twentieth century approached, Chamberlins was the city's most palatial store. There were separate departments for Manchester goods, haberdashery, hosiery, mantles and fancy goods, another for boots, clothing and cloth, and a dress department which claimed to 'stock every novelty as it comes out'. There was a mail order business, and an extensive wholesale trade.

Chamberlins continued the practice in the drapery trade of providing accommodation for staff. In 1881 there were 40 clerks, apprentices and drapery assistants living at the market place store, male and female. Perhaps surprisingly, even when the store was rebuilt after the fire the firm continued to provide accommodation. In 1901 nearly 30 were listed living there along with the cooks and domestic staff who cared for them.

Under the direction of Alexander and George there was no slackening in expansion. A large three-story extension and basement store at the rear of the building was opened in the spring of 1887. The popular Manchester goods and bales of calico were stored in the basement whilst the floors above provided additional sales space. Home furnishing occupied the first floor, shawls and haberdashery the second, with Bradford woollen goods on the third. The balustrades and fluted iron columns that supported them were painted in French grey with the firm's monogram picked out in chocolate on each panel. A new lift linked all the floors.

THE MOVE INTO MANUFACTURING

To meet the demands of their wholesale customers the brothers opened factories in Norwich. The largest was the clothing factory in Botolph Street, opened between 1877 and 1883 (it has been difficult to confirm the actual date). This turned out ready-made men's clothes to fill the orders brought in by the firm's travellers who scoured Norfolk, Suffolk, Cambridgeshire, Essex, Herfordshire and Lincolnshire for business.

The factory stood close to the junction with Calvert Street. It was evidently successful, as in 1903 a new factory, designed by A. F. Scott and described by architectural historian Nicholas Pevsner as 'the most interesting factory building in Norwich', was built on the same site. It had over 300,000 cubic feet of space and enough room to accommodate 1,000 workers. The electric-powered machines for sewing cloth, inserting eyelets, button holes and pockets were supplied from a dynamo in the basement supplied by Laurence Scott, which replaced the steam engine used by the old works. Much of the clothing made was uniforms and waterproof coats for the armed services and local volunteers, the Post Office, police and the railway companies.

The experience of making protective clothing was put to good use in 1912 when Chamberlins obtained the exclusive right to manufacture Pegamoid waterproofs. It was claimed the Pegamoid process ensured that garments treated with it were not affected by very high or very cold temperatures, did not deteriorate when in contact with grease or motor oil and did not blister. The coats were sold for various uses, including motoring and horse riding, but the largest demand was from the Admiralty who ordered 10,000 garments. During the latter part of that year, 300 of the factory's workers were turning out 250 Pegamoid coats a week. The overall workforce was about 600. It is unclear when production ceased at Botolph Street but Chamberlins had wholesale premises there until 1949 when the buildings were taken over by a printers.

There was a major change to the structure of the business in 1903 when it became a limited company, known as Chamberlins Ltd, and offered shares to the public. There was a share capital of £160,000 composed of preference and ordinary shares although only £140,000 were issued. There was also an offer of 4% debenture stock, redeemable in 1910. The Chamberlin family maintained control, announcing they would be taking up a quarter of the preference shares, nearly all of the ordinary shares and more than half the debentures. Several non-family members became directors of the new business including J. W. Bunting and the manager of the Botolph Street factory. At around this time the wholesale arrangements of Bunting and Chamberlins were amalgamated. J. W. Bunting would go on to become the General Manager of Chamberlins.

HALF A CENTURY'S SERVICE

The next few decades were ones of consolidation, punctuated by war and the deaths of the Chamberlin brothers. By the time George Chamberlin celebrated his fifty years with the firm in September 1911 there were nearly 1,000 employees. The First World War brought huge demand for military clothing and waterproofs which the Botolph Street factory worked flat out to meet, only to have the contracts terminated at the cessation of hostilities. Alexander died in June 1921 at The Grove in Ipswich Road – his home for many years. Like his father he had been civically active, serving as Mayor in 1892, but, although a member of the Conservative party, he was not politically active. His main interest was in church affairs and he was instrumental in the major restoration of the church of St Peter Mancroft, making a substantial donation toward the cost. He married Agnes Marshall, the daughter of London draper James Marshall, head of Marshall and Snelgrove, in 1863. The marriage produced two sons and two daughters.

George died seven years later in August 1928 aged 82. His passing marked the end of an era, the last of the larger than life figures who had dominated the city's commercial life for so long. He had entered his father's business at the age of 15 and remained active until a few days before his death at his home at St Catherines Close in All Saints Green. In addition to his role as the Managing Director of Chamberlins, he was the chairman of Buntings. For a period he was the Chairman and Managing Director of Swan and Edgar in London, a director of Boulton and Paul and of the Norwich Union Fire and Life Societies. He was active politically. Starting out as a Liberal he was first elected to the Norwich City Council in 1894 but subsequently joined the Conservative ranks, serving as Mayor in 1891, the year before his brother held the office, and as Lord Mayor in 1916, and again in 1918 when he was knighted. A rather austere man, quietly dignified and reserved with a brusque manner he had a number of homes before settling at St Catherines Close. When he lived at Bixley he was often seen riding into work early in the morning on horseback. His later years were marred by the tragic death of his daughter Gladys, killed when she was thrown from the car she was driving after it hit a bank near Kett's Oak at Wymondham.

Below: The Guildhall Hill store decorated for the Silver Jubilee of 1935.

Between the wars Chamberlins remained the city's pre-eminent department store. Their Christmas window displays in the mid-1920s were described as the best in Norwich, attracting crowds of window shoppers each evening. The store retained its reputation for quality and style well through the next decade and into the 1940s. Joyce Gurney-Read recorded her memories of Chamberlins; 'It was a pleasure to shop at Chamberlins in the thirties and forties. You were welcomed by a floor walker, who escorted you to the desired department. The little drawers under and behind the counters were filled with an amazing array of items for sale, all of which were displayed with great artistry on the counter for the customer's perusal. Chairs were provided for all to sit upon, and the goods selected were duly packed, and would be delivered to your home if required.'

Change came steadily following an opaque statement in the *Eastern Evening News* in August 1949 that 'the resources of Debenhams of London would be placed at the disposal of Buntings and Chamberlins of Norwich' – in other words they had been taken over. The new owners announced there would be no changes and the two stores would continue to trade under their existing names and management. This state of affairs didn't last long and in December 1954 Debenhams announced that as part of major refurbishment of the Guildhall Hill store it would be renamed Marshall and Snelgrove. The frontage of the store was to be altered and a restaurant opened within the store. The work was completed the following April and the new restaurant, with its red and cream decor, which seated 300, provided a panoramic view across the market place from the first floor over the main entrance.

The final act for the Guildhall Hill store came in May 1963 when Debenhams announced it was to close, that Marshall and Snelgrove would amalgamate with Garlands and trade from the London Street store from the following August. The store closed on the 1st August after a sale where much of the stock was sold at cost price. The building was later converted to offices and a supermarket.

CHAPTER 7

NORWICH'S OTHER INDUSTRIES

In addition to the major industries that dominated the commercial life of the city, by the end of the nineteenth century Norwich was home to a number of others, including the manufacture of men's and women's clothes, brush making, soap making and, perhaps somewhat surprisingly, cigar and cigarette making.

WHOLESALE CLOTHING

The clothing trade was dominated by F W Harmer & Company, reputedly one of the oldest clothing firms in the country, which began life in Norwich in 1825 when William Harmer entered into partnership with Samuel Rivett. Rivett retired in 1850 and William's grandson Frederick William Harmer took over the business. He would become the driving force behind the firm's expansion. By 1869 their

Bethel Street factory had over 200 employees making clothing for the wholesale trade, using steam-powered machinery for cutting cloth, sewing and making button holes to fill the orders garnered by Harmers commercial travellers.

Above: Harmer's factory in St Andrews Street before its destruction in 1943.
Left: Frederick William Harmer.

Finding the Bethel Street premises too cramped, a new factory, designed by Norwich architect E. T. Boardman and known as the 'St Andrew's Steam Clothing and Hosiery Works', was built on St Andrews Street. It could turn out 1,000 garments a day and was one of the first to be lit by electricity, supplied from dynamos provided by W. H. Scott in the adjoining Stamp Office Yard, although the machinery was steam powered. The works turned out shirts, collars, ties, braces, hats, caps, handkerchiefs and mufflers for men and sufficient children's garments 'to clothe every boy in East Anglia'. The firm was also quick to begin making made-to-measure suits for the middle class. Much of the women's clothing was outerwear – mantles, jackets, waterproofs and golf capes. Harmers also made waterproof garments under its own 'Monsoon' label.

The new factory employed around 1,500 people, 80% of whom were women and girls. They worked a 56-hour week, from 8 a.m. until 7 p.m. with an hour for dinner. Wages, as in many of the other Norwich factories, were low. Men averaged 28 shillings and four pence a week but women only ten shillings and nine pence. Later a factory was established at Heigham to make cardigan jackets, jerseys, shirts, pants and worsted hosiery. The firm also did a steady trade in converting ex-military greatcoats into cheap serviceable overcoats, sold to men who would otherwise have been without a warm winter coat. Some were renovated and sold as uniforms to the local volunteers (the equivalent of today's Territorial Army). This stood the firm in good stead when war came in 1914 when the St Andrew's factory went over to making clothing and uniforms for the Army and other government departments.

During the Second World War much of Harmer's production was again turned over to war needs, with over two million garments being made.

> Harmer's factory on St Andrews Street could turn out 1,000 garments a day and was one of the first to be lit by electricity.

Production was brutally interrupted in March 1943 when the St Andrews Street factory was hit by an incendiary bomb and completely destroyed. It resumed at a number of rented buildings until 1947 when a new factory was built at Mile Cross. By the time Harmers celebrated their 150th anniversary in 1975 it was one of the largest privately owned clothing manufacturers in the country, with branch factories at Diss, Fakenham, Stradbroke, Syleham and Watton. Sadly, this success was not to last and by 1990 the firm had gone into liquidation in the face of strong foreign competition and a depressed home market.

BRUSH MAKING

Brushes had been made in Norwich from at least the eighteenth century, using Norfolk timber to make the stocks and handles, and Russian bristle for the brushes. By 1890 there were at least 15 brush makers trading in the city. The largest was S. D. Page and Sons, one of the largest brush makers in the United Kingdom, employing 600 people in Norwich and at its recently opened factory at Wymondham. The Norwich factory dominated the Haymarket, with five floors packed with men and women making every conceivable type of brush for the wholesale trade.

Opposite:
Interior of
Harmer's factory
in 1948.

A 1904 account gives a vivid description of the Haymarket factory which was making everything from small domestic toilet brushes to large rotary brushes used for sweeping roads. The work was labour intensive, and required a high level of dexterity – especially when drawing the bristles through the stock to make the brush head. Traditionally, brush making was a male preserve but, following a series of strikes in the 1890s, women were increasingly employed and by 1904 there were almost 200 in the drawn department which occupied three floors at the Haymarket factory. The women worked at benches where the wooden stock was held in a vice and the women drew the bristles through pre-drilled holes using a thin copper wire. This process had replaced the traditional way of binding the bristles with boiling pitch or wire. Once complete a back would be put on the brush in the finishing department.

In the pan department the cheaper brooms were made much as they had been for years. Groups of men sat round a central container of boiling pitch with prepared bristles to hand. The bristles would be tied at one end and dipped in the pitch before being inserted into a hole in the broom stock. Paint brushes were also made individually. The handle was held in a vice before the bristles, which had been cemented together, were tightly wired to it. The finished brushes were then bleached, washed and dried, before being packed in tins for distribution.

THE WYMONDHAM WORKS

The Wymondham works, opened in 1886 in a row of cottages in Lady Lane, had a large timber yard with drying sheds and workshops where the stocks and handles were cut, turned, and pre-drilled to supply the Haymarket works. Using machines developed by the firm, there was an automated production line where the only work done by hand was the final polishing and finishing. Much of the workforce was female, brought in to operate the machines, but poorly paid compared with the men and the Norwich employees. Most of the wood used was grown locally. Alder, birch, oak, elm, chestnut and sycamore were all used but beech became the staple. Boar bristle imported from Russia was the other main raw material until the introduction of vegetable fibre in the mid-nineteenth century.

The founder of the business was Samuel Deyns. He was apprenticed as a basket maker in 1736, and later entered into partnership with a basket maker and osier grower (osier being a fast-growing tree whose wood was used in basket making) in the Haymarket before buying the business following his partner's death in 1762. Deyns later acquired larger premises there and the Haymarket would remain the company's base for over a century. In the early days the firm not only made baskets but traded as a brush maker, paper merchant and a manufacturer of clogs and pattens. Pattens were wooden overshoes, kept in place with straps, worn to protect the wearer's shoes from the muddy and unpaved streets of the time. In 1803, just before his death, Deyns took his son-in-law Samuel Deyns Page into partnership. He and his son, also named Samuel Deyns Page, would play an important role in the success of the firm, which became known as S. D. Page and Sons in 1860 when the younger Page brought two of his sons, Frederick John and Charles Fountain Page in as partners. By then Pages was well established. Their Haymarket factory had been extended to meet

the growing demand for all types of brushes and the number of employees had grown fivefold from the 20 or so employed in the early 1850s. Steam power had been installed to produce paper bags used by grocers, drapers, confectioners and other shopkeepers.

In the 1840s vegetable fibre became available and was used for making the cheaper brushes, replacing the more expensive bristle. The first type to be used was known as Bahia Bass, fibre stripped from under the bark of the palm tree and originating from Brazil. About a decade later Mexican fibre, taken from a cactus that grew only in one part of Northern Mexico, came into wide use. It was strong and hard wearing, able to retain liquid without losing rigidity, making it ideal for distemper and masonry brushes.

Opposite: S. D. Page & Son's factory on The Haymarket. Left: Charles Fountain Page. Below-left: Samuel Deyns Page.

Right: A former
brush factory
in St Georges
Street.

CONCENTRATING ON BRUSH MAKING

By the 1870s Pages had stopped turning out baskets and pattens to concentrate on making brushes, printing and papermaking, and selling stationery. The Haymarket works was not only producing thousands of paper bags but had begun printing headed stationery and advertising material for local businesses. Its brushes were sold at home and abroad, aided by a network of agents and commercial travellers which covered Britain and Ireland. The firm was also successful in winning contracts to supply local authorities and the armed services with brushes. This success was checked by the difficult conditions of the 1880s when a trade depression, the loss of foreign markets, and a huge increase in imports of cheap brushes – many made in foreign prisons and effectively dumped on the UK market – made life difficult for Page and Sons. As sales dropped wages were cut and piece-rate working reintroduced to reduce costs.

This proved insufficient to staunch the losses and the firm turned to large-scale mechanisation. This was resisted by the workforce, many of whom had spent their working lives developing the skills to make brushes by hand. Faced with the introduction of machinery, they feared for their jobs. After wage reductions in January 1891 the male brush workers went on strike and many were subsequently dismissed.

The years of depression also caused tension between Charles and Frederick Page who were now running the business. It was finally resolved when the business was split into two separate companies. The printing side moved to a new purpose-built works near St Stephen's Church to be known as Page Brothers and Company and run by Frederick Page. S. D. Page and Sons continued at the Haymarket, expanding brush making into the space left by the printing department, and becoming a limited company under the direction of Charles Page. Overcoming technical problems and resistance from the workforce, he introduced machines able to fill the stocks with a minimum of supervision, although as can be seen from the description of the works in 1904 there was still a large amount of skilled hand work. A second brush factory in Museum Court, off St Andrews Street, was opened in 1903 but was to close soon after the end of the First World War.

The war years proved to be a difficult time for the business but it was also a profitable one. The male workforce was heavily depleted as many enlisted. The cost of purchasing bristle, still used for the best quality brushes, soared and imported hardwoods became difficult to obtain. However, domestic sales rose with the absence of foreign competition and the firm benefitted from large government contracts although they were abruptly cancelled when peace came. Foreign imports, many from Germany, returned with a vengeance, taking up a large share of the English market and contributing to the closure of some English brush factories and a lack of orders at others. During the early 1920s Page's two factories were running at 50% of capacity, often working a three-day week.

By now the firm's brushes were sold under the 'Briton Brush' trade name. Recognising the benefits of being more closely identified with their brand, in 1920 S. D. Page and Sons became the Briton Brush Company. Later that year there was a merger with the long-established London brush makers D. Matthew and Sons. The new company, still known as Briton Brush, continued to struggle in the face of cheap foreign imports. In 1927 it was decided to close the Haymarket factory, ending 175 years of brush making there. Production was concentrated at Wymondham.

Briton Brush remained one of the leading firms in what was a small industry, concentrating on the manufacture of household and paint brushes, using vegetable fibres for the cheaper brushes and pig bristle for the better quality paint brushes. Taken over by the Reed Paper Group in 1967, the Wymondham factory was subsequently sold to the Windmill Brush Company which went into liquidation in 1982. The former factory in Norwich's Haymarket became the home of F. J. Lambert and Co, tobacco merchants, but was demolished in the 1960s to make way for a new C & A store.

SOAP MAKING

The city's textile industry had long been a heavy user of soap, supplied by manufacturers known as soap boilers. It was used to clean the yarn, which retained much of its original grease after it had been spun, and the finished cloth. Some cloth, known as 'grey' or 'white' was woven using unwashed yarn, with the cloth being washed before it was sent for dyeing and finishing. Where the yarn was to be dyed before being woven it would have been washed beforehand. This process would take place in the scouring houses of the master-weavers. Even after the industry began to decline there was a huge demand for soap in Norwich. By the mid-1840s 1.5 million pounds of soap was being made in Norwich by a small number of manufacturers – Bayne in his *History of the Trades and Industries of Norwich* says there were five at the time he was writing in 1852. Making the hard soap was a messy and smelly process, involving the boiling of wood ash and animal fat known as tallow, which was imported from Russia. The industry received a boost in 1853 when the long-standing tax on soap was repealed. Production flourished and within less than 20 years 300 million pounds of soap was being made in the Norwich Excise area, largely for use in the processing of silk, wool, linen, flax and cotton although there was also was an increasing demand for domestic soap.

One of the city's most well-known soap boilers was William Andrews who made soap for over 40 years at his works in Fishergate, on the east side of the road by the church of St Edmund. He had initially been in partnership with Robert French and others as soap boilers and crape manufacturers during the 1840s. The partnership was wound up in October 1855 and Andrews continued as a soap boiler and candle maker at the same site. He died suddenly at his Magdalen Street home one Sunday evening in May 1887 after complaining of a shortage of breath. At the time of his death he was one of only two soap manufacturers in Norwich. Within a few years there were none.

TOBACCO MANUFACTURING

One of the city's lesser but nevertheless interesting industries was tobacco. The raw material was processed and used in the making of cigars and cigarettes. For most of the nineteenth century there were several tobacco factories in Norwich with James Newbegin, who had a factory in the Bridewell and a shop on Guildhall Hill, the most well established. It was a difficult industry to succeed in. Tobacco was heavily taxed and the industry was strictly monitored by the Excise officers responsible for ensuring that the tax was collected and all the tobacco imported was accounted for.

By 1890 there was only one firm of tobacco manufacturers left in Norwich – Adcock and Son. They had their main premises in Queen Street and a shop at the Back of the Inns, but later moved production to a factory at 28 Pottergate, on the south side of the street between Upper Goat Lane and Fishers Lane. The business had been founded by Daniel Adcock who had arrived in Norwich in 1847 to manage James Newbegin's tobacco factory before going into partnership with Samuel Denham in 1868 as Adcock and Denham. If anybody could have been said to have been born to the trade it was Adcock. His father was a cigar maker in New York before the family returned to England, where Daniel entered the

tobacco trade in London. Upon Denham's death in 1885 Adcock became the sole proprietor. He later took his son Ernest into partnership, renaming the firm Adcock and Son. By then the firm was described as the largest tobacco manufacturers in the eastern counties and had a network of travellers bringing in orders. Ernest took no part in public life but was interested in art and was an accomplished painter. In 1903 he was one of the first people in Norwich to own a motor car, when he acquired a Wolseley.

The Pottergate factory was a substantial business, taking up three floors and employing large numbers of men and women. Almost all the tobacco used was imported from the United States, Cuba, the East Indies, China and Japan and arrived in leaf form in hogsheads, tierces and bales. Hogsheds and tierces were large wooden casks, a tierce holding the equivalent of 42 gallons, and bales came wrapped in jute. The finest cigars were rolled from Cuban tobacco, grown in the north west of the island. The tobacco leaf was first sorted into the various grades by size and colour before the stalk was stripped out. The stalks were milled into snuff which was returned to the Excise authorities for the tax on it to be reclaimed – duty had been paid on the whole imported bale or cask, which of course included the stalk. Some of the snuff was sold but it seems likely that most was destroyed.

Far left: The cigarette department at Adcock's factory in 1904.
Left: Daniel Adcock.
Opposite: Samuel Bignold.

The tobacco was then spun, heated, steamed, and cooled before being cut into strands of varying length according to its final use. Adcocks produced a wide range of tobacco products, including their own brand 'Black Prince' pipe tobacco and 'Sure Shot' cigars, of which 2,000,000 a year were being made in the early twentieth century. Although some of the cigars were made in moulds, all the cheroots and most of the cigars were hand rolled by the women employees.

In 1908 Ernest's son, Ernest Noel Adcock, joined the firm and under his direction the manufacture of cigars and cigarettes was superseded by the development of an extensive distributive trade. The firm continued in business in Norwich with its warehouse and shops until the late 1940s when the Pottergate premises were taken over by Palmer and Harvey and the shops closed.

The industries described here were not the only ones in Norwich during the nineteenth and early twentieth centuries. The city was also home to rope makers, carriage makers, bone merchants, building contractors, the largest monumental masons in East Anglia, and a maker of pianofortes. Also based here – although outside the scope of this book – were the services which supported the manufacturing industries. Of these the most important were the railways, insurance and banking.

THE RAILWAYS

The coming of the railways in 1844 had revolutionised the transport of goods – allowing raw materials to be brought to Norwich quickly, cheaply and in bulk, and facilitating the rapid distribution of the finished goods across the United Kingdom and further afield. The railway companies, the Great Eastern in particular, were also major employers and much of their engineering work was undertaken in Norwich.

INSURANCE

The provision of fire and life insurance would become intrinsically associated with Norwich as Norwich Union Fire and Life Societies became nationally successful under the direction of Samuel Bignold and his successors. The societies swelling coffers also provided funds for some of the local industries – Norwich Union had a long term relationship with brewers Steward & Pattesson for one.

BANKING

The story of the city's banks was not such a successful one, littered as it was with a series of bankruptcies and frauds culminating in the catastrophic collapse of the Crown Bank in 1870. The one exception was the Gurney Bank which survived successfully before being subsumed into the newly launched Barclays in 1896.

NORWICH INDUSTRIES TODAY

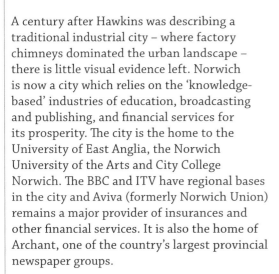

A century after Hawkins was describing a traditional industrial city – where factory chimneys dominated the urban landscape – there is little visual evidence left. Norwich is now a city which relies on the 'knowledge-based' industries of education, broadcasting and publishing, and financial services for its prosperity. The city is the home to the University of East Anglia, the Norwich University of the Arts and City College Norwich. The BBC and ITV have regional bases in the city and Aviva (formerly Norwich Union) remains a major provider of insurances and other financial services. It is also the home of Archant, one of the country's largest provincial newspaper groups.

However, Norwich still makes things. The former Bayer CropScience factory, now owned by Aurelius, employs over 200 people making crop protection chemicals. Double glazing, at one time the great post-war success story in Norwich, is still produced, although not on such a large scale as formerly. The city is home to a major bottle top and fastener company and water heaters have been made in Norwich since 1920.

A few survivors of the city's traditional industries still remain. Unilever's Carrow factory still produces Colman's mustard. Van Dal continues to manufacture women's shoes at its Dibden Road factory using traditional methods combined with modern materials. Perhaps the most successful survivor is ATB Laurence Scott, a leader in the manufacture of bespoke electric motors, continuing a tradition started by W.H. Scott in King Street.

For the careful observer there are reminders of the city's lost industries – Boulton and Paul's former offices in Rose Lane is now a housing development, the former shoe factory in St Marys Plain once used by Sexton, Son and Everard has a diverse range of uses whilst much of Bullard's Anchor brewery forms part of the Anchor Quay residential scheme.

Although Norwich's heyday in manufacturing may have passed, its industries have consistently innovated over the years, moving from textile production to shoe-making as the former declined, inventing new technologies and products, and branching out into the creative and knowledge sectors – the city continues to develop, thrive and innovate.

BIBLIOGRAPHY

Ashwin, T. and Davison, A. 2005. *An Historical Atlas of Norfolk*. Stroud: Phillimore

Ayers, B. 2009. *Norwich – Archaeology of a Fine City*. Gloucester: Amberley

Bayne, A. D. 1852. *An Account of the Industries and Trade of Norwich*. Norwich: Norfolk Chronicle

Barber, A.-M. 2008. *Ephraim Hinde – Silk Weaver*. Norwich: Unpublished

Barfield, T. 1968. *Scott Built a Dynamo*. Norwich: Privately published.

Barringer, C. 1984. *Norwich in the Nineteenth Century*. Norwich: Gliddon Books

Bayne, A. 1869. *A Comprehensive History of Norwich*. Norwich: Jarrold and Sons

Boulton and Paul. 1947. *The Leaf and the Tree*. Norwich: Boulton and Paul

Briers, F. (ed.) 1961. *Norwich and its Region*. British Association for the Advancement of Science: London

Bullard, H. H. 1902. *Sir Harry Bullard MP*. Norwich: Goose

Bullard Family Scrapbook, c. 1880

Burgess, E. & W. 1905. *Men who have made Norwich*. Norwich: Burgess

Butt, J. J. 2001. *The Transaction of privilege in medieval urban society – a study of the English brewers*. Ann Arbour, Michigan: UMI

Chapman, K. 1986. *The Breweries of Norwich*. Norwich: Unpublished

Clark, C. 2004. *Work and Employment, Norwich Since 1550*. London: Hambledon and London

Clark, C. 1996. *A Brush with Heritage – The History of Hamilton Acorn*. Norwich: CEAS

Day, M. 2010. *Brewing in Norwich*. Norwich: Norfolk Museums and Archaeology Service

Donovan, R. 2009/10. *Drink in Victorian Norwich – Brewery History 130,132, 143*. Brewery History Society

Edgar, S. 1994. *Colmans of Norwich – A Short History*. Norwich: Unpublished

Fowler, E. 1962. *A Hundred Years in the Shoe Trade 1862-1962*. Norwich: Jarrold

Gourvish, T. 1978. *Norfolk Beer from English Barley*. Norwich: CEAS

Grocer, The. 1862 *Mustard and Starch – a day at the Carrow Works, Norwich*. The Grocer: London

Gurney-Read, J. 1988. *Trades and Industries of Norwich*. Norwich: Gliddon Books

Hancock, T. 1873. *Norwich Industries*. Norwich: British Association

Hawkins, C. B. 1910. *Norwich: A Social Study*. London: Philip Lee Warner

Hickling, R. G. 1882. *The Life of Harry Bullard*. Norwich: RG Hickling

Hinde, Fras & Sons. 1947. *The Story of Norwich Silks*. Norwich: Fras. Hinde & Sons

Holmes, K. 1992. *Two Centuries of Shoemaking: Start-rite 1972-1992*. Norwich: Start-rite

Jarrold and Sons. 1910. *Citizens of No Mean City*. Norwich: Jarrold and Sons

Jennings, P. February 2009. *Liquor Licensing –and the Local historian: the 1904 Licensing Act*. British Association for Local History

Jennings, P. May 2010. *Liquor Licensing and the local historian: inn and alehouses*. British Association for Local History

Jennings, P. May 2011. *Liquor Licensing and the Local historian: the Victorian public house*. British Association for Local History

Johnson, J. H. Undated. *Norfolk Scrapbook Vol 3*.

Johnson, M. 2008. *The Norwich Shoe Industry 1850-1900*. Norwich: Norwich Industrial Archaeology Society Journal Vol 8 No 3

Jones, D. 1986. *Business, Tact and Thoroughness: A History of the Novic Shoe Company* Norwich: Norwich Industrial Archaeology Society Journal Vol 4 No 1

Martins, S. W. 1984. *A History of Norfolk*. Chichester: Phillimore

Morris, T. 2008. *Made in Norwich – 700 Years of Textile Heritage*. Norwich: Nick Williams

Morris, C. (ed.). 1947. *The Journeys of Celia Fiennes*. London: Cresset Press

Morton, V. 1984. *The Nineteenth Century – Colmans and Norwich*. Milton Keynes: OU Press

Rudd, W. A. 1923. *The Norfolk & Norwich Silk Industry – Norfolk Archaeology Volume 21*. Norwich: Norfolk & Norwich Archaeological Society

Sparks, W. L. 1949. *The Story of Shoemaking in Norwich*. Northampton: National Institute of the Boot and Shoe Industry.

Tillett, E. A. 1900. *Norwich Scrapbooks Volume 17*.

Walpole, J. 2011. *Alehouse Keepers of King Street in the Seventeenth and Eighteenth Centuries*. Norwich: Unpublished

Wheldon, F. W. 1946. *A Norvic Century*. Norwich: Jarrold & Sons

Wilson, R. 2004. *The Textile Industry, Norwich Since 1550*. London: Hambledon & London

Yaxley, P. 1991. *Wymondham's Old Inns*. Wymondham: Wymondham Historical Society

Directories:

Harrod. 1877. *Royal County Directory of Norfolk with Lowestoft in Suffolk* Norwich: G. Harrod & Co

Hunt, E. 1850. *Directory of East Norfolk, with part of Suffolk*. London: E. Hunt & Co

Peck.T, 1801. *The Norwich Directory*. Norwich: J. Payne

Pigot. 1830. *National Commercial Directory*. London: Pigot & Co

Pigot. 1839. *Directory, Norfolk [and] Suffolk*. London: Pigot & Co

White, F. 1854. *History, Gazetteer, and Directory of Norfolk, and the City and County of Norwich*. Sheffield: F. White & Co

White, W. 1883. *History, Gazetteer and Directory of Norfolk, including the city of Norwich*. Sheffield: William White

White, W. 1890. *History, Gazetteer and Directory of Norfolk, including the city of Norwich*. Sheffield: William White

Winton, M. 1991. *Chase's Norwich Directory 1783*.

Newspapers:

Norfolk Chronicle
Norwich Mercury
Eastern Daily Press
Norwich Evening News
Times Online

Journals:

Journal of the Norfolk Industrial Archaeology Society

INDEX

PHOTOGRAPHY AND ILLUSTRATIONS

Picture Norfolk

Page 9: Norwich from St Peter Mancroft; page 15: James Churchyard; page 16: Hindes silk cloth; page 18: Charles Hinde; page 19: Hindes dyeing silk cloth; and Hindes factory floor; page 21: Howlett and White clicking floor; page 23: Howlett and White interior; page 26: Howlett and White; Haldenstein and Bally shoe factory; page 34: Factory on St Peters Street; page 35: Bernard Hanly; page 36: Southall factory; page 43: Youngs, Crawshay and Youngs' King Street brewery; page 48: the Anchor brewery; page 49: Richard Bullard; page 50: Harry Bullard; page 51: Bullard coopers; page 52: the chimney at the Anchor brewery; page 55: Bullard directors; page 56: filling the barrels at Anchor brewery; page 62: making chocolate by hand at Caleys; page 70: Carrow works; page 72: die stamping the penny tins at Carrow; page 74: scraping starch at Carrow; page 75: Colman's starch advert; page 82: Barnards wire netting; wire weavers at Barnards; page 83: Barnard's Norfolk Iron Works; page 86: Holme's Prospect Place works; page 87: Boulton and Paul aeroplane; page 89: Boulton and Paul's Riverside works; page 99: William Harding Scott in his office; page 101: the Gothic Works; page 102: Laurence Scott pattern shop; Laurence Scott foundry; page 109: Buntings store; page 113: site of Curls; page 116: bomb damage at Buntings; page 119: Silver Jubilee Garland's London Street store; page 120: Garlands after the fire; page 126: Chamberlin's Guildhall Hill store illustration; page 131: Harmer's factory in St Andrew's Street; page 133: interior of Harmer's factory; page 134: S. D. Page & Son's factory; page 139: Samuel Bignold.
Images courtesy of Norfolk Library and Information Services – to view thousands of images of Norfolk's history visit www.picture.norfolk.gov.uk.

George Plunkett

Page 13: Weaving sheds to rear of Magdalen Street; page 37: Steward and Patteson's Pockthorpe brewery; page 44: offices at Steward and Patteson's Pockthorpe brewery; page 68: Caley's factory; page 121: Bond's Ber Street store; page 125: Butcher's draper's shop; page 130: Silver Jubilee Chamberlin's store on Guildhall hill; page 136: former brush factory.
Photographs © George and Jonathan Plunkett – www.georgeplunkett.co.uk.

Archant

Page 44: Morgan's brewery trucks; page 46: Watney's brewery; page 76: Phillipa Flowerday; page 78: Robinson's soft drinks; page 93: Autowrappers; page 95: overhead view of Balding Engineering; workshop at Balding Engineering; page 97: construction of Beaver Engineering factory; page 98: Diamond H Controls; page 106: Laurence Scott; page 117: Garland's advertisement.
Photographs © Archant CM Ltd – Norfolk.

Other photographs belong to the author Nick Williams and HEART.

Photographs on page 31: Charles Winter; page 33: James Southall, Southall Factory; page 53: Anchor brewery engineer's shop, fermenting tuns; page 128: showroom, drapery department at Chamberlins; page 135: Charles Fountain, Samuel Deyns Page; page 138: Adcock's cigarette department, Daniel Adcock – are from Burgess, E. & W. 1905. *Men who have made Norwich*.

Photographs on page 71: Jeremiah Colman, and page 77: Jeremiah James Colman, are from *A Souvenir of the Centenary of J&J Colman*, Ltd: 1805–1905, Norfolk News Co Ltd, 1905.

Photographs on page 33: Bernard Hanly; page 61: advertisements; page 65: Read's flour; page 66: Henry Robertson; page 111: Henley Curl; page 115: Charles Arthur Bunting; John Walter Bunting; page 117: Garland's advertisement; Richard Garland; page 118: Frank Garland; page 122 Bond's advertisement; Robert Herne Bond; page 128: Chamberlin's Botolph Street factory; page 131: Frederick William Harmer – are from *Citizens of No Mean City*, Jarrold & Sons, 1910.

Illustrations – page 10: power looms, from Williams, Nick. *St James Mill, Norwich*, Jarrold & Sons, 2012; page 93: Barnard's advertisement, from *Barnard's Journal*, 1953.

THE TEXTILE INDUSTRY

01 Former weaving shed at rear of 24-28 Magdalen Street

02 St James Mill, Whitefriars

FRANCIS HINDES

03 Site of St Mary's Mill, Oak Street

04 Site of first Hinde's factory, St Augustines

BOOT AND SHOE-MAKING

05 Former Norvic shoe factory, St Georges Plain

06 Former Haldenstein's shoe factory, Queen Street

07 Former Sexton Son and Everard shoe factory, St Marys Plain

08 Van Dal shoe factory, Dibden Road

START-RITE

09 Site of former Start-rite factory, Crome Road

10 Site of James Smith's shop and Southall factory, St Peters Street

BREWING

11 Former offices of Steward and Patteson, Silver Road

12 Former Crown brewery of Youngs, Crawshay and Youngs, King Street

13 Site of Morgans/Watneys brewery, King Street

BULLARD & SONS

14 Former Anchor brewery, Coslany Street

FOOD MANUFACTURING

15 Site of former Hills and Underwood vinegar brewery, Prince of Wales Road

16 Site of former Caley/Mackintosh chocolate factory, Chapelfield

17 Albion Mill, King Street

18 Site of former Wincarnis works, Barn Road

19 Former offices of Smith and Sons, Magdalen Street

COLMAN'S OF CARROW

20 Carrow Works, Bracondale

21 Former Colman's School, Carrow Hill

22 Colman's Mustard Shop & Museum, Royal Arcade

ENGINEERING

23 Coslany Bridge

24 Former Boulton and Paul offices, Rose Lane

25 Site of Barnard's Norfolk Iron Works, Coslany Street

26 Former Holmes/Pank's showroom, Cattle Market Street

27 Former site of Boulton and Paul's Riverside works, Riverside

LAURENCE, SCOTT & ELECTROMOTORS

28 Gothic Works, Hardy Road

29 Site of former Thorpe Road works

THE NORWICH DRAPERS

30 Former Bunting's store (now Marks & Spencer), Rampant Horse Street

31 Former Curl brothers' store (now Debenhams), Red Lion Street

32 Site of former Garlands store, London Street

33 Former Bond's store (now John Lewis), All Saints Green

34 Site of former Henry Jarvis store, St Benedicts Street

35 Former Butcher's store, Bedford Street

CHAMBERLINS

36 Former Chamberlin's store, Guildhall Hill

37 Site of former Chamberlin's factory, Botolph Street

NORWICH'S OTHER INDUSTRIES

38 Site of former Harmer's factory, St Andrews Street

39 Site of former Page brush factory, Haymarket

40 Site of former Andrews' soapworks, Fishergate

41 Site of former Adcocks tobacco factory, Pottergate

KEY

■ Existing buildings   ▨ No longer existing buildings

Only places within easy access of the city centre are included, so sites such as Barnards on Salhouse Road and Diamond H at Mile Cross are not shown.

ACKNOWLEDGEMENTS

As someone who grew up with neighbours who worked in breweries, engineering works and shoe factories, it seems little has been done to mark the passing of these industries. This is a modest attempt to do that, recalling the trades and firms that employed thousands of people within recent memory and sent Norwich-made goods across the world.

I have received help and advice from many people in carrying out the research and writing of this book. I am particularly grateful to the following: Maggie Johnson, Thelma Morris, Colin Marney, Mary Fewster, the staff at both the Norfolk Heritage Centre and the Norfolk Record Office, Rosemary Dixon (the librarian) at Archant, and Clare Everitt at Picture Norfolk. I must also thank my colleagues at HEART, Michael Loveday, Lindsey Roffe and Janet Robertson who have made this book possible. Finally, thanks must go to my wife Gill for her help and forbearance.

Left: Norwich's skyline today – note the absence of chimneys compared with the photograph on page 9.